PRINTED ON RECYCLED PAPER

Changes in Your World

STEVE PARKER

QED Publishing

Consultant: Terry Jennings
Project Editor: Anya Wilson
Design and Picture Research: Dynamo Design

Copyright © QED Publishing 2010

First published in the UK in 2010 by
QED Publishing
A Quarto Group Company
226 City Road
London EC1V 2TT
www.qed-publishing.co.uk

All rights reserved. No part of this publication may be reproduced, stored in a retrieval system, or transmitted in any form or by any means, electronic, mechanical, photocopying, recording, or otherwise, without the prior permission of the publisher, nor be otherwise circulated in any form of binding or cover other than that in which it is published and without a similar condition being imposed on the subsequent purchaser.

ISBN 978 1 84835 422 7

Printed in China

Picture credits

(t=top, b=bottom, l=left, r=right, c=centre, fc=front cover)

6–7: Hywit Dimyadi/Shutterstock; 6: b Phase4Photography/Shutterstock, t Pepita/Shutterstock, l Martine Oger/Shutterstock, br Peter Blottman/Shutterstock; 7: t Andreas Maeyer, lb Nikolay Okhitin/Shutterstock, r kkaplin/Shutterstock, br Tischenko Irina/Shutterstock; 8: l Dr Morley Read/Shutterstock, b Vincent Laforet/Pool/Corbis; 9: r Hugo de Wolf/Shutterstock, b Galyna Andrushko/Shutterstock, br Hirlesteanu Constantin-Ciprian/ Shutterstock; 10–11: Alex Staroseltsev/ Shutterstock; 11: r patrimonio/ Shutterstock; 12–13: Serg Zastavkin/ Shutterstock; 12: br Andrey Pavlov/Shutterstock; 13: br Peter Zaharov/Shutterstock; 14–15: Mark William Richardson/ Shutterstock; 14: r yanik Chauvin/Shutterstock; 15: t nmedia/Shutterstock; 16: br Tom Grundy/ Shutterstock; 17: br Yvan/Shutterstock, tr Clin Keates/Getty; 16–17: Stephen Aaron Rees/Shutterstock; 18–19: Andrei Merkulov/ Shutterstock; 18: t syba/Shutterstock, l Stefen Redel; 19: tr Dean Mitchell/Shutterstock, br Norman Pogson/ Shutterstock; 20: l Kurt De Bruyn/ Shutterstock, br Tyler Olson/Shutterstock, b Jason Hawkes/Getty; 21: tr Stephen Finn/ Shutterstock, l Leah-Anne Thompson/ Shutterstock, br David Roos/Shutterstock; 22–23: Dan Knitwood/staff/Getty; 22: t Mikael Damkier/ Shutterstock, bl Tyler Olson/ Shutterstock; 23: br David Hyde/ Shutterstock, tr Tariq Dajani/Getty; 24–25: US Air Force/ Science Faction/Getty; 24: b Burma News Agency/Corbis; 25: br Enika Balogh/ Shutterstock, tr NASA; 26–27: Marco Simoni/Corbis; 26: l Ashley Cooper/Corbis; 28–29: Elena Elisseeva/Shutterstock; 28: r italianestro/ Shutterstock; 29: r Destiny VisPro/Shutterstock, tr Tim Pannell/Corbis, b Kevin Dodge/Corbis; 30: t Stanislav Popov/ Shutterstock, l iofoto/ Shutterstock, r Rafa Irusta/ Shutterstock, b Bryan Buscoicki/ Shutterstock, br Terrance Emerson/Shutterstock; 31: bl AFP/Stringer/Getty, t Terry W Eggers/Corbis; 34–35: Hywit Dimyadi/Shutterstock; 34: l David B Fleetham/Photolibrary, t Phase4Photography/ Shutterstock, r Kitch Bain/Shutterstock, b Mike Powles/Photolibrary; 35: b DLILLC/Corbis, tr Tischenko Irina/Shutterstock, cr: Dwight Smith/Shutterstock, c fenghui/ Shutterstock; 36–37: c Kaspars Grinvalds/Shutterstock; 36: t sabri deniz kizil/Shutterstock, b Norma Cornes/Shutterstock; 37: t Jason Hawkes/Getty, b Pichugin Dmitry/Shutterstock; 38–39: c Photolibrary; 38: l amygdala imagery/Shutterstock; 39tr Frank Greenaway/Getty; 40–41: Crom/Shutterstock; 40: c Cordelia Molloy/ SPL, t LoopAll/Shutterstock, r iofoto/Shutterstock, b Dario Sabljak/Shutterstock; 41: tr James P Blair/Getty; 42: c Jeff Foott/Getty, b iofoto/Shutterstock, br Jame Hager/Getty; 43: c Johnny Lye/Shutterstock, t M Harvey ABPL/Photolibrary; 44–45: c Richard du Toit/Getty; 44: b D H Webster/ Photolibrary; 45: t LUC GNAGO Reuters/Corbis, b Pallava Bagla/Corbis; 46–47: c Reuters/Corbis; 46: bl imageshunter, br tkemot/Shutterstock; 47: tr Barbara Peacock/Getty, b Dean Murray Illustration Shutterstock, br Natalie Forbes/Getty; 48: cl Keiichi Takita/Getty, cr Michael Langford/Getty, b Nick Garbutt/NHPA; 49: tr Jack Picone/Alamy, c Michael G Smith/Shutterstock, bl Borislav Gnjidic/Shutterstock, br Elena Eliseeva/Shutterstock, b matt/ Shutterstock; 50–51: c Flip Nicklin/FLPA; 50: b INGO ARNDT/FLPA; 51: cr Joel Sartore/Getty, t EcoPrint/Shutterstock, tr Spectra/Shutterstock; 52–53: c Tony Crocetta/NHPA; 52: t Andy Crawford/DK, l jan kranendonk/ Shutterstock, c Sam Chadwick/Shutterstock; 53: br Francoise De Mulder/Getty, l Lynsey Allan/Shutterstock, t Ngo Thye Aun/Shutterrstock, tr Ruta Saulyte Laurinaviciene/Shutterstock; 54: c China Photos/Getty, br Michael Latz/Getty, t Laurent Renault/Shutterstock, c Gina Buss/Shutterstock; 55: br Mike Dunning/DK, tl sabri deniz kizil/Shutterstock, t Kim Worrell/Shutterstock; 56–57: c George Antoni Hemis/Corbis; 56: r Daniel Heulcin/NHPA; 57: br ANT Photo Library/NHPA, t hagit berkovich/Shutterstock; 58–59: c Andrejs pidjass/Shutterstock; 58: tr Inc/Shutterstock, c Konstantin Sutyagin/Shutterstock, cr STILLFX/Shutterstock, 59: br Nigel Hicks/NHPA, t Eric Gevaert/Shutterstock, l Charles Taylor/Shutterstock; 62–63: c Hywit Dimyadi/Shutterstock; 62: l Peter Jackson/ Bridgeman, br Peter Jackson/Bridgeman, c Phase4Phtography/Shutterstock, t Pepita; 63: r Justin Bailie/Getty, tr Lebrecht Authors/Alamy, b Stephen Mcsweeny; 64–65: c VisionsofAmerica/ Joe Sohm/Getty; 65: tr Pers-Anders Pettersson/Getty, b China Photos/Getty; 66–67: c Orientaly/Shutterstock; 66: bl yxowert/Shutterstock; 67: tr szefei/Shutterstock, br Kevin Britland/Shutterstock; 68–69: t CROM/Shutterstock; c David Lee/Shutterstock; 68: l Semen Lixodeev/Shutterstock; 69: br 0399778584/Shutterstock, b Steffen Thalemann/Getty; 70–71: c Philippe Barseiller/Getty; 70: bl Scott Stulberg/Getty, b Andrew Holt/ Getty; 71: cr Frank Gaglione/Getty, br Kevin Schafer/Getty; 72–73: c Stuart McCall/Getty; 72: bl Kevin Schafer/Alamy; 73: tl Frontpage/Shutterstock; 74–75: c Mircea BEZERGHEANU/Shutterstock; 74: b Lakis Fourouklas/Shutterstock; 75: bl Ron Sherman/Getty, tr Angelo Garibaldi/Shutterstock; 76: bl Gerard Loucel/Getty, r Svetlana Gajic/Shutterstock; 77: c Travel Ink/Getty, b Mark Anderson/Getty, tr Dean Mitchell/Shutterstock; 78–79: c Peter Anderson; 78: bl Mark Yuill/Shutterstock; 79: tr John Lund/Matt Holmes, br Guryanov Oleg/Shutterstock; 80–81: c Hein van der Heuvel/Getty; 81: b Stockbyte/Getty, tr Paula Gent/Shutterstock, c amlet/Shutterstock, r R Perreault/Shutterstock; 82–83: c Dave Reede; 82: l Frontpage/Shutterstock; 83: tr Peter Dazeley, b Luis Velga; 84: bl Jan Butchofsky-Houser/Corbis, r Tim Multon/Alamy, br Miglbauer Hans/Alamy; 85: Chris Sattlberger, t Terry W Eggers/Corbis; 86–87: c Finbarr O'Reilly/Corbis; 86: l matka_Wariatka/Shutterstock, l Sven Hoppe/Shutterstock, b Maria Sauh/Shutterstock; 87: tr David Sutherland/ Getty, br Marcus Prior/WFP/Corbis; 90–91: t sjgh/Shutterstock, c Ilja Masik/Shutterstock; 90: l sandra zverlein/ Shutterstock, tr kwest/Shutterstock; 91: tr Lagui/Shutterstock; 92–93: c Hywit Dinyadi/Shutterstock; 92: t flashfilm/Getty, t Phase4Photography/ Shutterstock, t Pepita/Shutterstock, tr mashe/Shutterstock, bl IKO/Shutterstock, b Mausinda/Shutterstock; 93: l Andrew Holt/Getty, b Andrew Hobbs/Getty, c Wendy Chan/Getty, tr Tischenko Irina/Shutterstock, t kazberry/Shutterstock; 94–95: t Kirsty Pargeter; 94: l David Davis/Shutterstock; 95: l Dmytro Korolov/Shutterstock, br Kharidehal Abhirama Ashwin/Shutterstock; 96–97: c Markusson Photo/Getty; 97: tr Yann Layma/Getty, bl Jens Mayer/Shutterstock, br ratluk/Shutterstock; 98–99: c Milton Wordley/Photolibrary; 99: bl Mediacolor's/Alamy, tr Ellen McKnight/Alamy, br Jacek Chabraszewski/Shutterstock; 100–101: c James P Blair/Getty; 101: t Ronald Sumners/Shutterstock, c Brian A Jackson/Shutterstock, br Otmar Smit/Shutterstock; 102–103: c Mitchell Funk/Getty; 102: bl Carlos Spottorno/Getty, t Christolph Weihs/Shutterstock; 103: t Oscar Schnell/Shutterstock, b Adrian Baras/Shutterstock; 104–105: c Corbis; 104: c Bengt Erwald/Getty, bl Ian Mckinnel/Getty, t Robyn Mackenzie/Shutterstock, t Germany Feng/Shutterstock, tr jocicalek/Shutterstock, b djslavic/Shutterstock; 105: t Lasevsky Pavel/Shutterstock, r Dragan Trifunovic/Shutterstock, bl David Hyde/Shutterstock, br max blain/ Shutterstock; 106: c Michael Blann/Getty; 107: t Steffen Koerster Photography/Shutterstock, br Hank Frentz/Shutterstock; 108–109: c Eddie Hironaka/Getty; 108: bl Noah Clayton/Getty, tr John Lock/Shutterstock; 109: t Hisham Ibrahim/Getty, b TNT Magazine/Alamy; 110–11: c Peter Chadwick/ SPL; 111: br Jonathan & Angela Scott/NHPA, tl Alistair Michael Thomas/Shutterstock, tr Stephen Bonk/Shutterstock; 112: c Jeff Zaruba/Getty, b Julio Etchart/Alamy; 113: tr Frederic Courbet/Getty, r Davis Marsden/Photolibrary, tr Mikael Damkier/Shutterstock, c Hugo Maes/Shutterstock; 114: bl G. Brad Lewis/Getty, br G Brad Lewis, tr Morgan Lane Photography/ Shutterstock;115: t Stephen Strathdee, l stocklight/Shutterstock, br Mateo_Pearson/Shutterstock

The words in **bold** are explained in the Glossary on page 116.

Contents

Climate
What is weather?	6
Climate change	8
Global greenhouse	10
A time of change	12
Climate culprits	14
Fossil fuels	16
Burning fuels	18
Greenhouse gases	20
Changing world	22
Weather warning	24
Rising sea levels	26
Slow the change	28
Keep it cool	30

Animal habitats
World of wildlife	34
People problem	36
Habitats galore	38
The biggest loss	40
Saving wild places	42
Food for us	44
Too much pollution	46
Warning! Invaders!	48
World famous	50
Tourists and pets	52
Captive breeding	54
Success stories	56
Help us!	58

Food and Farming
Down on the farm	62
Growing food	64
Fertile land	66
Farming wood	68
Nature in danger	70
Double disaster	72
Make way for farms	74
Endless fields	76
Hi-tech farming	78
Farming the sea	80
Energy farms	82
Mountains and miles	84
Keeping shelves full	86

Population
Only one world	90
Footprints	92
Plenty of people	94
Raw materials	96
Energy to burn	98
Warmer world	100
Going places	102
House and home	104
Watch that waste!	106
Food and health	108
Losing wild places	110
Fairtrade	112
Be aware!	114
Glossary	116
Index	119

CLIMATE

Our climate has been changing. Temperatures are becoming warmer, which has a big impact on wildlife. Read on to find out how your small changes can make a big difference.

What is weather?

When you wake up in the morning, the first thing you notice is the weather! Hot, cold, sunshine or rain – weather can change every day.

Some places have extreme weather. A snowfall covers everything in sight.

Changing weather

There is a huge range of weather around the world. Some places have more calm periods than others, or more or less sunshine, cloud, rain, wind, snow or ice. They have more or fewer storms, **floods** and **droughts**. In some places, weather conditions change quickly. There might be freezing fog, then warm sunshine, then clouds and rain, all in one day!

Hurricanes can flood whole cities, causing serious damage to people's homes.

🎧 Satellite pictures show the swirling air of hurricanes. from high above the Earth.

Woolly mammoths died out about 4000 years ago.

FOCUS ON

Ice Ages

Climates have changed many times in the past. During ice ages the whole world was much colder. The last Ice Age started about 50,000 years ago and finished 10,000 years ago. In frozen northern lands, woolly mammoths and rhinos had thick fur coats to protect them from the cold.

Climates

Weather is what happens day by day. **Climate** is the average weather conditions over a much longer time – years and centuries. A **tropical** climate is hot all of the time. A **polar** climate is very cold most of the time.

⬆ In a polar climate, there is snow and ice all year round.

⬅ In a tropical, dry climate, there is hot sunshine for most of the day.

CLIMATE change

The Earth has different climate areas, or zones. There are different zones around the North Pole, South Pole and near the Equator.

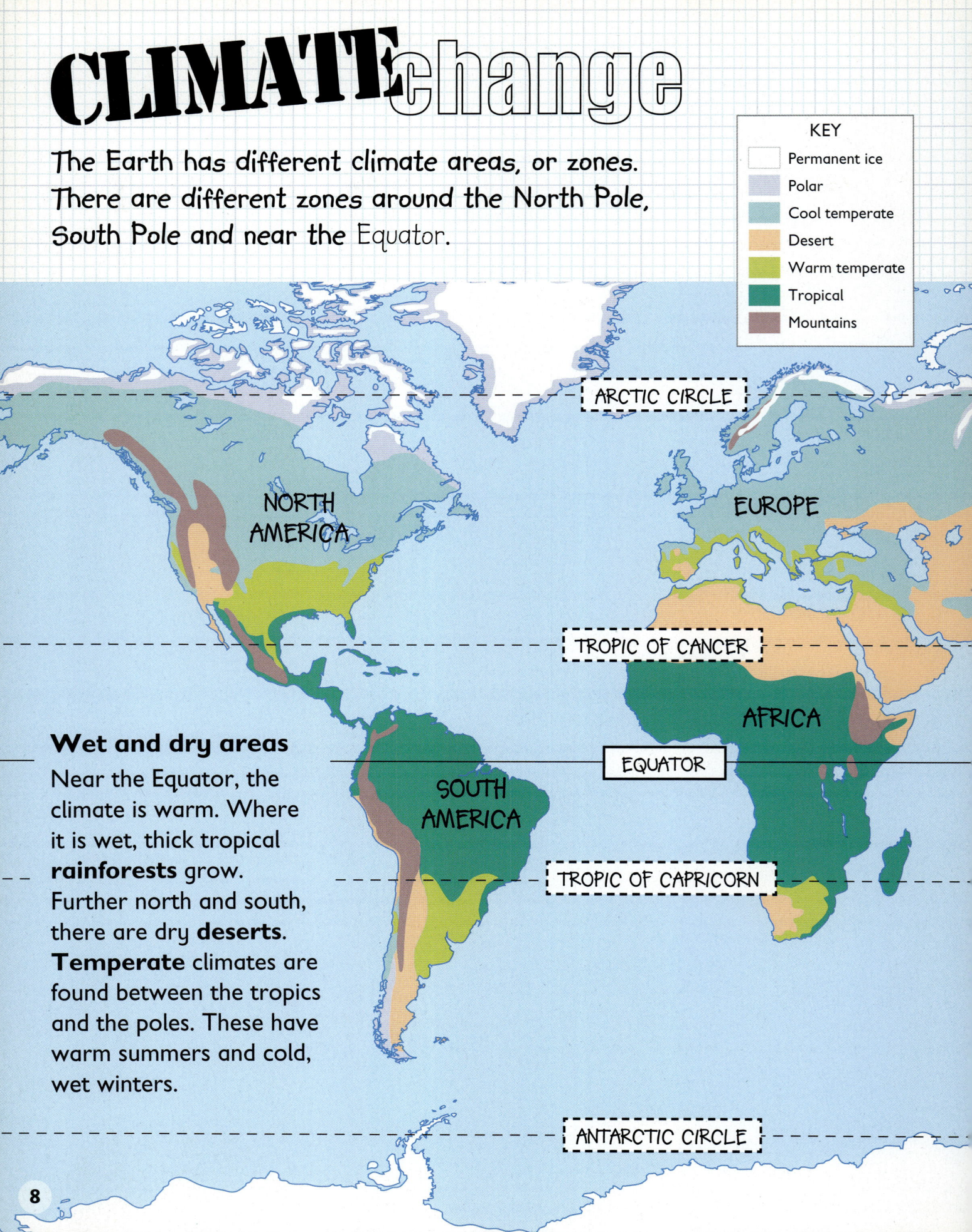

KEY
- Permanent ice
- Polar
- Cool temperate
- Desert
- Warm temperate
- Tropical
- Mountains

Wet and dry areas

Near the Equator, the climate is warm. Where it is wet, thick tropical **rainforests** grow. Further north and south, there are dry **deserts**. **Temperate** climates are found between the tropics and the poles. These have warm summers and cold, wet winters.

⮞ The closer an area is to the Equator, the hotter the temperature is because the Sun's rays are more direct.

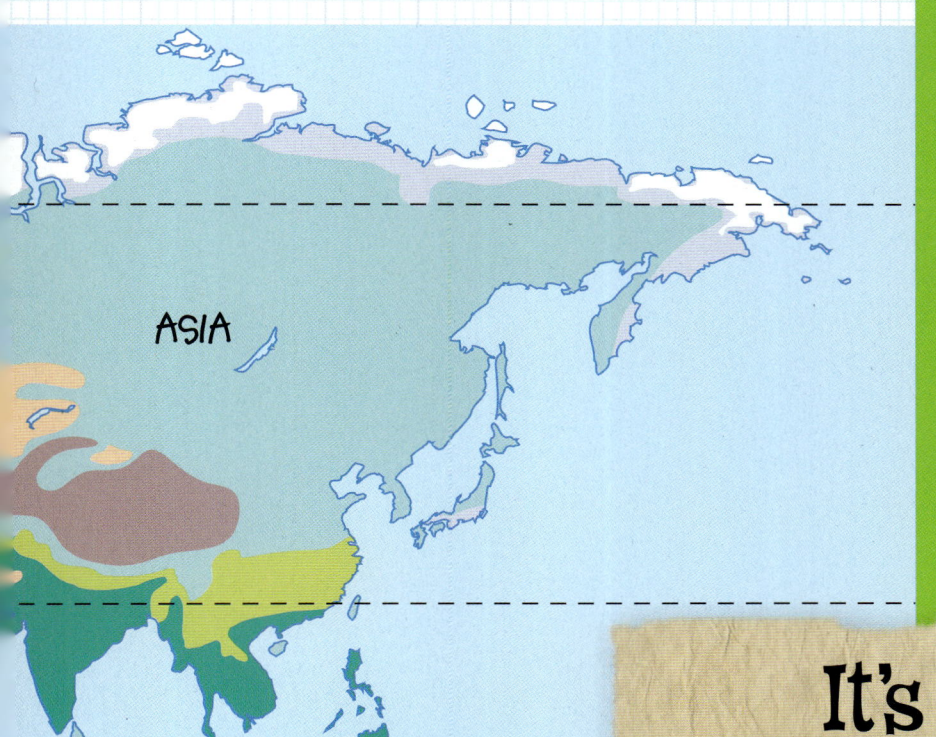

Rays are spread out away from the Equator

Rays are focused at the Equator

Sun's rays

North Pole / Tropic of Cancer / Equator / Tropic of Capricorn / South Pole

Cold and hot regions

Tropical regions are warmest. The Sun is high above and its strong rays beat straight down. Polar regions are coldest. In the far north and south, the Sun is low in the sky, even at midday. Its rays are spread over a wide angle, so their heat is spread over a much greater area.

ASIA

OCEANIA

🎧 The coloured areas show different world climate zones on land. The climate at sea may be windier and less rainy than on land.

ANTARCTICA

It's a wonder!

In the hottest deserts, almost no life can survive.

The average temperature in the Arctic during winter is about -30 degrees Celsius.

Temperature measures hot and cold. Most people feel comfortable at 21–22 degrees Celsius. The hottest temperature ever recorded was in Libya, Africa – almost 58 degrees Celsius. The coldest was on Antarctica – -89 degrees Celsius.

Global greenhouse

A greenhouse has a clear glass roof and walls. Inside, it is usually warmer than outside, especially on a sunny day. This is because the glass traps heat from the Sun inside the greenhouse. The air that surrounds the Earth acts in the same way as the glass in a greenhouse.

Keeping in heat

The layer of air around the Earth is called the atmosphere. It lets most of the Sun's rays pass through it, to the Earth's surface. The atmosphere also traps some of the heat from these rays, stopping them from escaping into space. This trapped heat keeps the Earth warm. This is called the greenhouse effect.

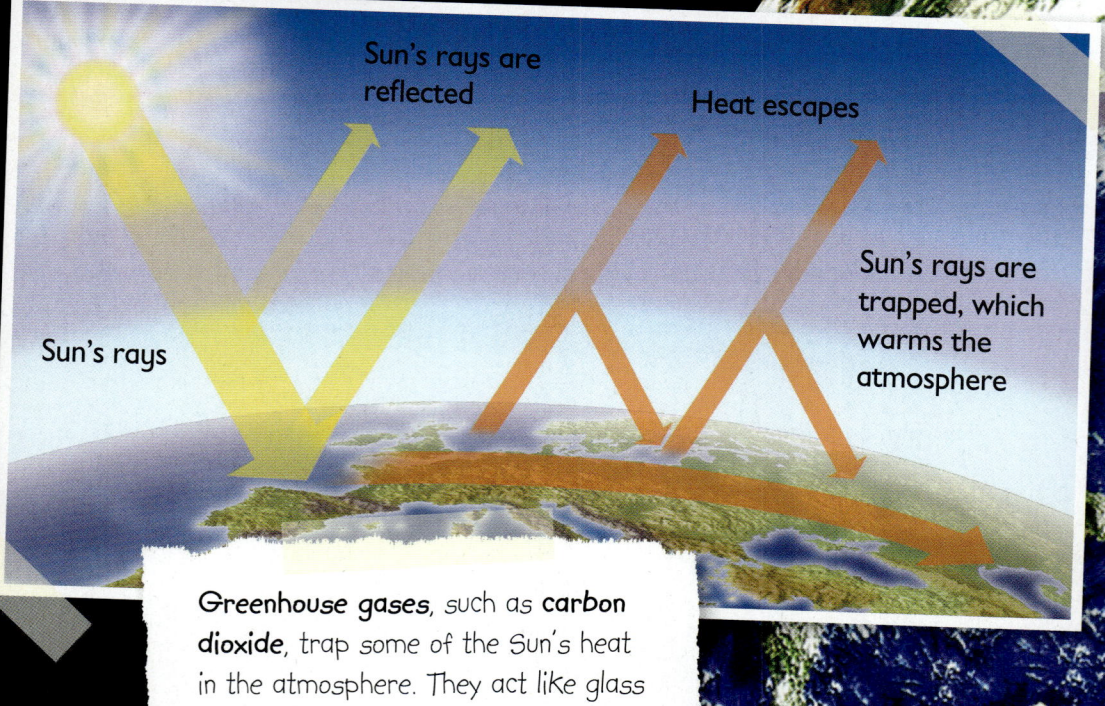

Sun's rays are reflected

Heat escapes

Sun's rays are trapped, which warms the atmosphere

Sun's rays

Greenhouse gases, such as **carbon dioxide**, trap some of the Sun's heat in the atmosphere. They act like glass in a greenhouse.

Natural balance

The Earth's natural greenhouse effect has been working for millions of years. With it, the average world temperature is 15 degrees Celsius. Without it, the temperature would be less than 0 degrees Celsius, with ice almost everywhere. The problem today is that we are altering the natural balance of the Earth's greenhouse effect.

↻ The atmosphere stretches to about 100 kilometres above the Earth — that's more than 330 Eiffel Towers high!

It's a wonder!

Venus is far too hot for any form of life to survive there.

The Earth is not the only planet with a greenhouse effect. On Venus, temperatures can reach up to 480 degrees Celsius. This is so hot that a piece of wood would catch fire by itself!

A time of change

For centuries, scientists have measured temperatures and other weather conditions on Earth. These conditions are changing, which is having a great effect on nature.

Global warming

Temperatures are measured daily, at thousands of weather stations worldwide, from high in the mountains to far out at sea. The results show that, almost everywhere, the Earth's climate is slowly getting hotter. Average temperatures are rising and the world is warmer than it was 100 years ago. This is called **global warming**. If this continues, in 100 years, Earth will be a very different place.

Researchers measure temperatures around the world, including at the poles.

➲ Weather stations vary in size, from a small box to a big building. They measure many weather conditions, including temperature, rainfall, wind and sunshine.

Nature knows

The natural world shows signs of global warming, too. Flowers come out earlier because winter becomes spring sooner. This also means that they die sooner and animals that normally feed on them are left with no food. Insects that were only found in the hot tropics are spreading around the world – and carrying dangerous **diseases** such as malaria with them. In cold places, ice sheets and glaciers are melting.

⇧ Flowers such as daffodils are coming out earlier each year, when there is still snow on the ground.

FOCUS ON

Glaciers

Rivers of ice are called glaciers. They flow very slowly down high mountain slopes and in cold lands. They usually move about 1-2 metres a year. Due to global warming, glaciers are starting to melt. In the future, this could cause low-lying land to flood.

Where glaciers meet the sea, chunks of ice break off as icebergs. As this ice melts, sea levels rise.

Climate culprits

The reason that the Earth is getting warmer is that we are changing its 'glass' – the gases that surround it. The natural greenhouse effect is becoming unbalanced.

Greenhouse gases

Earth's atmosphere is made of a mixture of gases. One is **oxygen**, which we need to breathe to stay alive. Another is **water vapour**, one of the main natural greenhouse gases. It soaks up the Sun's heat and holds onto it. Water vapour can make the air feel moist and clammy.

Wht Cn U do? Turn off lights when they're not being used. This saves electricity, so power stations don't need to make as much.

⊙ Smoke, fumes and vapours from power stations add to the greenhouse gases in the air.

Too much

One very important greenhouse gas is carbon dioxide. It forms only a tiny amount of the atmosphere. However, the amount is rising, mainly because when we burn fuels such as coal, petrol, gas and wood, we make carbon dioxide. Its global warming effects are powerful.

🔊 Water vapour in the air turns into tiny water droplets, which form clouds.

It's a wonder!

Scientists use weather balloons to measure temperature and the amount of water vapour in the air.

Many of the warmest years measured by scientists have been in the past 15 years. Almost everywhere in the world, the climate is changing.

Fossil fuels

Fossil fuels are coal, oil and natural gas, and fuels made from them, such as petrol and diesel. They contain a substance called carbon. When carbon burns, it forms the greenhouse gas carbon dioxide.

In the rocks

A **fossil** is the remains of something once alive, such as an animal or plant, preserved in the rocks. Fossils take millions of years to form. Many fossils have been found, including giant shark teeth and plants.

⊃ Fossils have formed from all kinds of dead materials, such as dinosaur bones.

1. The dinosaur dies and its soft parts rot away.
2. Sand and mud bury the hard bone.
3. More layers collect on top as the bones turn to stone.

Coal, oil and gas

Lumps of coal are the hard, black fossil remains of giant plants that grew on Earth more than 300 million years ago. Thick, sticky oil in the ground is the remains of tiny sea creatures and plants that also lived millions of years ago. Natural gas deep underground was made in a similar way to oil, but it became a gas, not a liquid.

Oil rigs at sea hold giant drills that reach oil deep under the seabed.

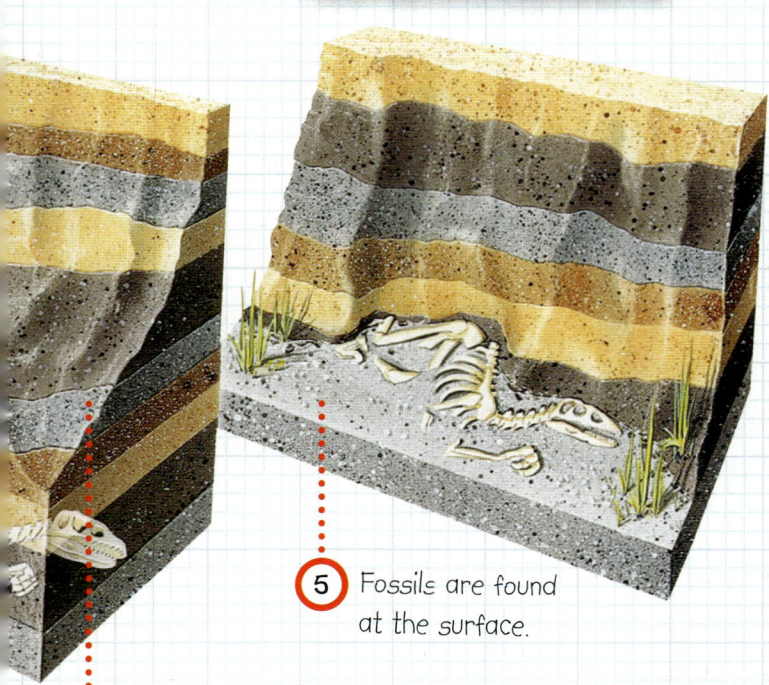

(4) Rocks are worn away by weather and earth movement.

(5) Fossils are found at the surface.

It's a wonder!

Next time you see a lump of coal, ask an adult to split it open. You may see shapes of leaves – these are fossils from millions of years ago.

Coal can contain fossilized animals and plants, such as fern leaves.

17

Burning fuels

Every day, people around the world burn large amounts of fossil fuels. This produces huge quantities of carbon dioxide. It also uses up fossil fuels we cannot replace.

↻ When factories make new products, such as plastic containers, they burn fuel to run the machinery.

Turn down the central heating slightly. It uses less fuel, makes less greenhouse gas – and saves money!

Wht Cn U do?

Energy and heat

Fuels contain lots of energy. Burning them releases this energy as heat. We use this heat in many ways — warming our homes, in the engines of cars and other vehicles, in aeroplane jet engines, in **power stations** to produce electricity and in factories to make products such as paper, glass and steel.

Two problems

Our modern way of life depends on burning fossil fuels. However, there are two problems. One problem is that they emit, or give off, carbon dioxide, which adds to global warming. The other problem is that fossil fuels are running out. We use them millions of times faster than they can form. If we keep using oil at the present rate, in 100 years there will be almost none left.

Vehicle engines use fossil fuels and pollute the air.

19

Greenhouse gases

Carbon emissions produced when we burn fossil fuels cause up to one quarter of the global warming effect. Other greenhouse gases include methane and ozone.

Smelly methane

Methane is part of natural gas. It's also made by cows when they digest food. It comes out of their mouths and their rear ends. As we raise more cattle, they put more methane into the atmosphere. Methane is also produced by rotting rubbish heaps and landfills. Methane causes up to one-seventh of global warming.

At landfill sites, huge pits are dug in the ground and the waste is buried.

You can usually find somewhere to recycle near your house.

Repair, reuse and recycle. This way, you save raw materials and energy, cause less **pollution** and reduce the rubbish in landfills.

In some cities, there is a layer of **smog** sitting in the air.

Ozone

Ozone is a form of oxygen. When strong sunlight shines on exhaust fumes from cars, ozone forms and can make it hard for us to breathe. However, high in the sky ozone is useful. A layer of ozone protects the Earth from the harmful rays of the Sun. **Manmade chemicals** are destroying this ozone layer.

Changing world

As global warming causes the climate to change, our world will alter in many ways. Scientists believe that there will be other problems besides warmer weather.

Farms and food

Changing climates will also affect our farms and food. Regions that grow vast fields of wheat, corn and other crops could become too wet or dry. As **grasslands** dry out, cattle and other farm animals could starve. In the sea, changes in water temperature mean there are fewer fish, so we cannot catch as many as we have been.

Cutting down trees destroys natural habitats, and affects the climate because trees take in harmful carbon dioxide.

In dry countries, people have to dig very deep wells to find water, and pump it to the surface. Water may become more scarce in the future.

📷 FOCUS ON

El Niño

Every few years, the waters and atmosphere of the Pacific Ocean undergo a change called El Niño. This produces many effects, from bigger storms to smaller fish catches. No one knows how climate change will affect El Niño.

When El Niño takes place, there are more storms and extreme weather.

Climate zones

Places that used to be rainy might get drier. Places that were once dry could be wetter. Some regions might get hotter, but a few could be cooler. As lakes dry out and deserts flood, wild animals and plants will face huge problems.

↶ Climate change could mean that farmland will become hard and dry.

WEATHER warning

As climates change, there may be more extreme weather, such as storms, floods, hurricanes, heatwaves and droughts.

Stormy weather

Over the last few years, there have been more hurricanes and other big storms around the world. As oceans get warmer, the storms become bigger, with stronger winds and more rain.

Hurricane Katrina filled the streets of New Orleans, USA, with water.

Heating up

On average, heatwaves and droughts are increasing. The Aral Sea in Central Asia and Lake Chad in Africa are just two watery places that are shrinking fast. People around them take water for their homes, factories and farms. If climate change continues to make land drier around the world, the need for water will increase.

🎧 *Between 1989 and 2003, the Aral Sea in Uzbekistan and Kazakhstan, Asia, dried out to less than half its size.*

Destruction

In 2005, Hurricane Katrina flooded the city of New Orleans, USA. In 2008, Cyclone Nargis flooded a massive area of Burma. More than 150,000 people died. High winds wreck buildings, and floods ruin farmland and cities.

It's a wonder!

Hurricane Katrina's fastest winds were 280 kilometres an hour, which is 2.5 times the motorway speed limit!

Rising sea levels

Global warming means that seas and oceans will get warmer. When things get warmer they expand, or get bigger. As the sea expands, the water level will rise.

Flood warning

Sea levels rise each year by one to 2 millimetres — almost the height of this 'o'. In the next 100 years they could rise more than one metre. That's enough to flood huge coastal ports and cities, and large amounts of low-lying farmland near the shore.

Since 1997, Tepukasavilivili Island in the Pacific Ocean has started to disappear because sea levels are rising.

Every minute, lumps of glaciers melt into the sea, making water levels rise.

Ice reflects many of the Sun's rays back into space

Light and heat rays hit ice

Ice

Sea

Water takes in heat and reflects fewer rays

As ice melts, less of the Sun's heat goes back into space, and global warming speeds up.

FOCUS ON

Mirror effect

Shiny white snow and ice reflect, or bounce back, the Sun's light and heat. As they melt, they reflect less of the Sun's rays. The heat stays in the atmosphere, which adds to global warming.

Melting ice

Melting ice also affects sea levels. There are massive amounts of ice in the towering glaciers and icebergs of Alaska, Greenland and Siberia in the north, and even more in Antarctica in the south. If it all melted tomorrow, sea levels around the world would rise by more than 50 metres.

Slow the change

There are many ways we can help to reduce global warming and slow climate change. If we all play a small part, it will add up to make a big difference.

Green solution

Carbon dioxide is good for plants. All plants need to take it in from the atmosphere. They combine it with energy from sunlight, to live and grow and make fruits and seeds. This process is called photosynthesis.

◉ *Plants take in excess carbon dioxide and give out oxygen, so they are very important to the environment.*

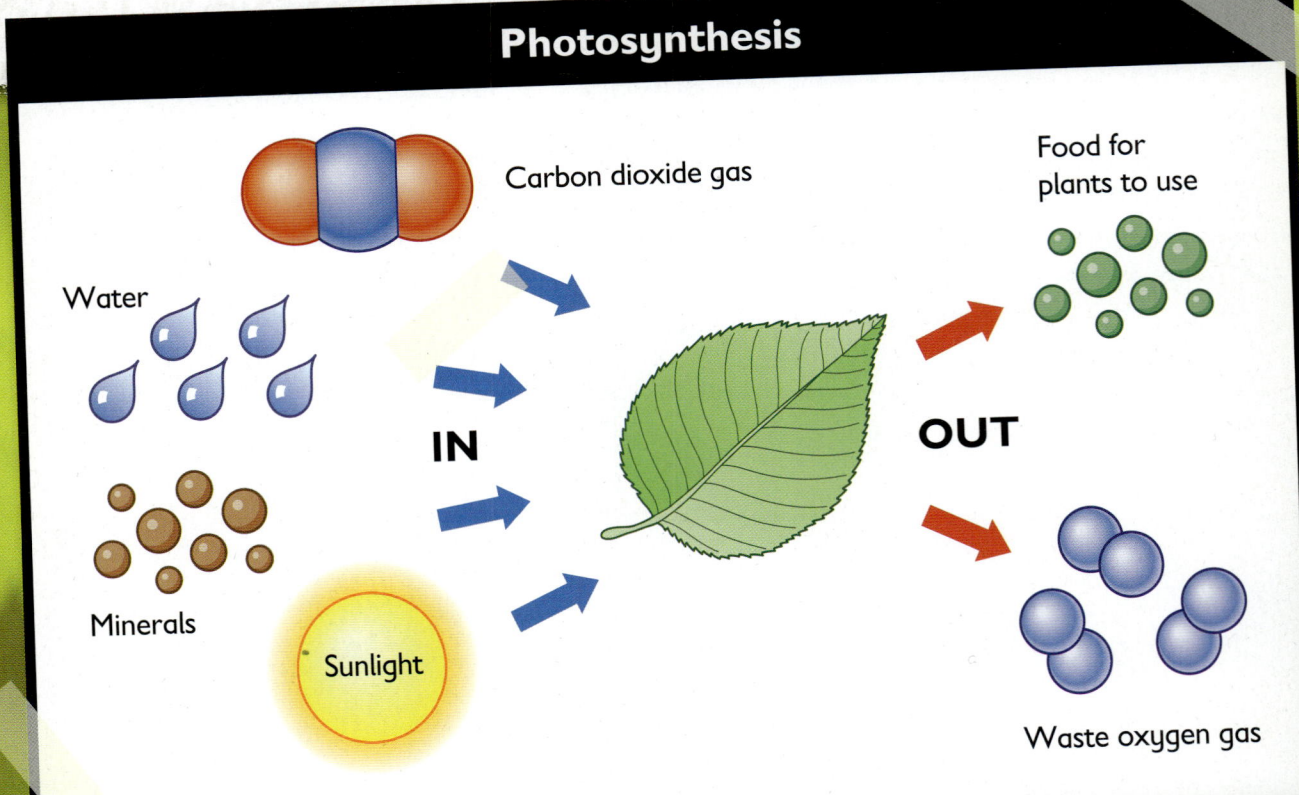

Photosynthesis

IN: Carbon dioxide gas, Water, Minerals, Sunlight

OUT: Food for plants to use, Waste oxygen gas

More means less

The more trees and other plants we have, the more carbon dioxide they use up, so the less there is for global warming. As we cut down trees, the opposite happens. This is why it's important to save woodlands, forests and other natural places, and to plant more trees.

⮕ The carbon cycle shows how carbon is constantly used and reproduced. By cutting down trees, the cycle becomes unbalanced.

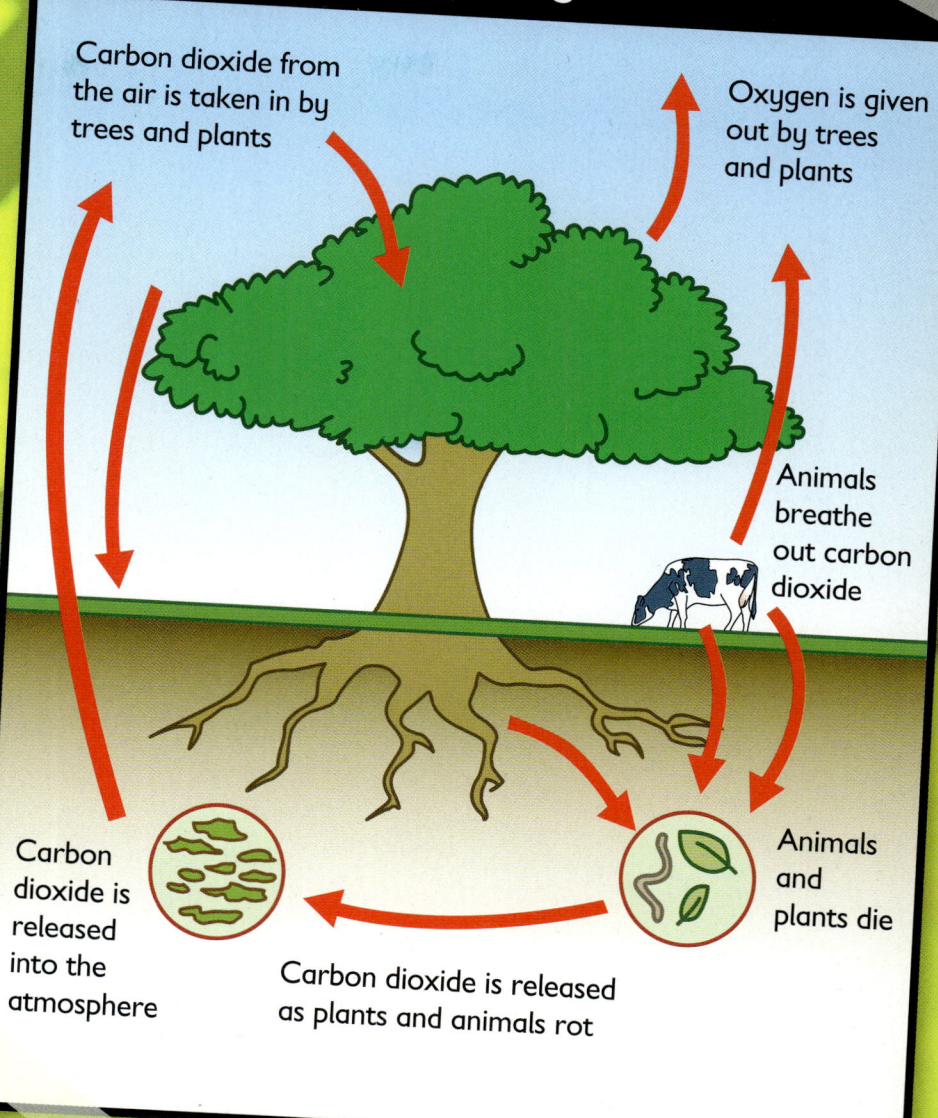

Carbon cycle

- Carbon dioxide from the air is taken in by trees and plants
- Oxygen is given out by trees and plants
- Animals breathe out carbon dioxide
- Animals and plants die
- Carbon dioxide is released as plants and animals rot
- Carbon dioxide is released into the atmosphere

Cycle, walk or take the bus or train, rather than a car.

Wht Cn U do?

Keep it cool

Most scientists agree that global warming and climate change have begun, and we must act fast to make it slow down.

◯ Wind is a free, long-term source of energy for electricity.

Hydroelectricity produces no greenhouse gases or pollution.

Alternative electricity

Two-thirds of the world's electricity comes from burning fossil fuels. We can support **alternative energy**, such as hydroelectric dams and wind turbines. **Nuclear power** stations produce little carbon dioxide, but they create other problems such as dangerous **radioactive** waste.

◯ The Hoover Dam on the border of Arizona and Nevada, USA, works by using huge generators. The generators are powered using the water.

A farmers' market sells local fresh produce. The food does not travel far.

- Buying food grown locally is one way to reduce our carbon footprint and travel miles.
- 'Carbon footprint' shows the carbon emissions a particular lifestyle produces.
- 'Travel miles' show how far goods and products travel, which produces carbon emissions.

Be aware

We must learn about global warming and try to change the way we live before it is too late. Governments and industries are trying to find ways to produce everything we need without harming the planet.

 **FOCUS ON**

Biofuels

Crops can be used to make fuel for vehicles – called **biofuel**. The plants take in carbon dioxide as they grow and burning the fuel produces it. Some people do not support biofuel production because either trees are cut down to grow the crop or the farmland could be used to grow food crops.

Corn is often harvested to create biofuel.

31

ANIMAL HABITATS

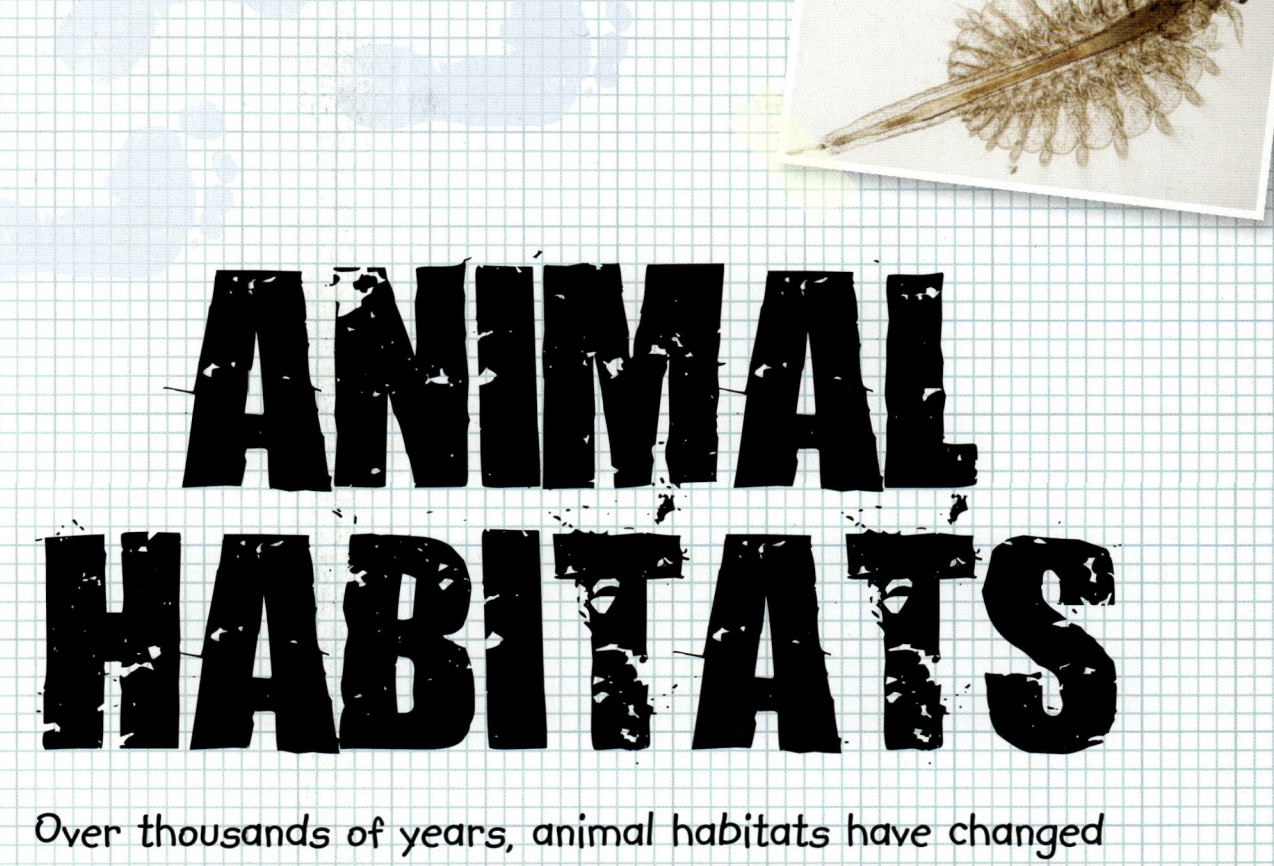

Over thousands of years, animal habitats have changed — some as a result of natural events, others have been destroyed by pollution and other human activity. Read on to find out how you can help to slow down these changes.

WORLD OF wildlife

Almost everywhere on Earth, there is wildlife. In tropical forests, monkeys swing through giant trees. On coral reefs, colourful fish dart away from sharks. On the African grasslands, elephants watch as lions stalk zebras.

⬆ The great white shark lives in the warmer waters of all the main oceans.

Orang-utans spend much of their lives in trees.

Survival everywhere

Even in the harshest conditions, wildlife survives. Among icebergs, polar bears use their warm fur coats to keep out the cold. In deserts, animals such as lizards hide away during the day to keep cool.

Elephants live in large family groups.

FOCUS ON

Fossils

The remains of dead animals and plants preserved in rocks are called fossils. They show that over millions of years, living things change. Some die away and new ones appear. Giant dragonflies, dinosaurs, sabre-tooth cats and mammoths have all disappeared over time.

↷ Fossils help scientists to discover what wildlife was like long ago.

↶ The number of giant pandas is growing — there are now more than 2000 in the wild.

A big problem

An amazing range of animals and plants live all around our world. Some are common, such as cockroaches and rats. Some are **rare**, such as giant pandas and tigers. The main problem for this wonderful variety of wildlife is people, who are destroying areas where they live. This may cause many **species** to become **extinct**.

The tiger is an **endangered** species. Only 4000 are left in the wild.

35

People problem

Every hour, 10,000 babies are born around the world – enough to fill 20 jumbo jets! These people all need somewhere to live.

◊ Every year, millions of houses are built on once-natural land.

More and more

As the number of people on Earth grows, so does the amount of things we need to live. People need food, from farms or fished from the sea. We produce things such as cars, televisions and other machines, in factories. We build ever-growing cities and towns, use huge amounts of electricity and travel around the world on holiday. We are using up the world's resources, and wildlife can suffer as a result.

It's a wonder!

People need electricity, but power stations can pollute the environment.

100 years ago there were 1700 million people in the world. Today there are more than 6700 million – four times more!

Effects on nature

Around the world, wild animals and plants are squeezed into smaller areas as people cut down trees or build on their **habitats**. This leaves wildlife with fewer places to live. Plants have less space to grow, which means that animals have less to eat.

As more roads and cities are built, woodland areas become smaller.

FOCUS ON

How many?

On farms worldwide, we have 1800 million sheep and goats, 1400 million cows and 1000 million pigs. The most common wild animal of similar size is the crabeater seal of Antarctica, with about 30 million.

Crabeater seals live in big groups. They feed on shrimp-like krill.

Habitats galore

You wouldn't expect to see a shark in a desert, or a dolphin on a mountain. Different animals and plants live in different natural places on Earth, called habitats. Some habitats are in more danger than others.

Different conditions

Some habitats are on land, others are in water. Land habitats may be a tropical rainforest or a mountain, a marsh or a desert. Water habitats can be very different temperatures, too — icy cold oceans or warm seas. The water can be fresh or salty.

Desert cactus plants have prickles to stop animals from eating them.

Survival

There is a huge variety of habitats. Wildlife can survive in different conditions. Over time, they have learned to feed on the food available, and their bodies have **adapted** to suit the habitat. Animals on snowy mountains, such as bears, have thick fur coats, and seabirds such as penguins have waterproof feathers and can swim.

It's a wonder!

Brine shrimps eat very tiny plants and animals.

A hot, salty lake is an extreme habitat. The water is 40°C – like a hot bath! Yet tiny creatures called brine shrimps can live there comfortably.

◅ Penguins have a thick, fatty layer of blubber under their skin to keep them warm in freezing temperatures.

The biggest loss

Habitat loss is the greatest problem for wildlife. As the world fills with more people and more towns are built, natural places where so many plants and animals thrive are lost forever.

Natural change

Habitats change naturally over time, and wildlife adapts in order to survive. In one place, heavy rain fills a valley so it becomes a new lake. Somewhere else, an earthquake cracks open the ground and makes a new valley. These changes have been happening for millions of years.

At Thingvellir, Iceland, a new valley is forming as cliffs move further apart every year.

Unnatural change

Today habitat change is different. Whole habitats are being wiped out by people — by building towns, farms, roads, shopping malls, factories and airports. Taking over a habitat means its plants and animals are lost, unless we give them somewhere else to live.

◖ Airports need a lot of space, which means less space for wildlife.

FOCUS ON

Tropical forests

In tropical forests it's warm all year. These places are 'hot spots' for the largest range of plants and animals. This variety of wildlife is called **biodiversity**. In the past 100 years, we have destroyed more than half of the world's tropical forests for timber and farmland because warm conditions are best for growing farm crops.

This tropical forest in Borneo was replaced by cacao trees, which are used to make chocolate.

Wht Cn U do?

Think about your own habitat. How much waste do you produce every day? Reuse toys rather than buying new ones, and recycle products such as paper and plastic. Then, fewer products have to be produced and habitats will not be destroyed by new roads and factories.

Coal is an important fuel for humans, but mining it can destroy natural areas.

SAVING wild places

Rare animals and plants can be kept in zoos and gardens. Without somewhere natural to live, they are never truly wild and free.

Somewhere to live
To save animals and plants, we must **conserve** the wild places where they live. The best way is to set aside places to be used as wildlife parks and **nature reserves**. Here, people must respect the wildlife, stay in certain areas and cause no harm.

Beavers live in rivers, and need clean water. They are easily harmed by pollution.

⊃ People observing wildlife in nature reserves, such as wildebeest in Africa, need to make sure they cause no harm.

Wht Cn U do?
Find out if there's a nature reserve in your area. Write a letter or send an email to find out how you can help.

Safe habitats

In a protected area, many living things, from big **predators** to tiny flowers, can thrive. More reserves and parks are set up every year.

⊂ Big animals such as moose, or elk, need huge areas to to roam and feed.

It's a wonder!

The world's largest nature reserve also has the longest name – Papahanaumokuakea. It covers several of the Hawaiian islands and the sea around them, in the Pacific Ocean.

Marine nature reserves help to protect wildlife such as the unicorn fish.

Papahanaumokuakea
Marine National Monument

Northwestern Hawaiian Islands
PACIFIC OCEAN

Food for us

Grassland provides food for many creatures such as elephants, zebras and bison. However, we also need it to feed our cows, sheep and other farm animals.

Not enough room

Farms are taking over huge areas of nature. Trees are cut down, plants are **ploughed** up and wild animals are driven away. Farm crops need water, which is taken from lakes and rivers, leaving less for fish and other wildlife. Crops are sprayed with **chemicals** to kill pests such as caterpillars. These chemicals affect other animals such as birds and butterflies. People also fish in the sea. As we take more fish for us to eat, seals, dolphins and seabirds have less food.

It's a wonder!

Every minute, an area almost the size of a football pitch is changed from natural land to farmland.

⤺ Bushmeat markets are very common, especially in Africa.

FOCUS ON 📷

Bushmeat

In some places, people hunt wild animals, to eat themselves or sell at the market. This meat is called bushmeat. Rare creatures such as monkeys, deer and wild pigs are often hunted for bushmeat, so are in great danger of extinction.

Ways to help

Scientists are developing new kinds of **crop** that need less water and fewer chemicals to help them grow. These crops can then be grown in more areas. Fishing nets can be designed to catch only certain kinds of fish, and let other creatures go.

⤴ New kinds of crops, such as these rice plants, can grow easily in dry weather.

45

Too much pollution

When harmful *substances* collect where they should not be, it is called pollution. It can range from litter in woodlands and on *beaches* to a giant oil spill out in the ocean.

Pollution we see

Some pollution is easily seen, such as small, factory oil spills in a river, harming fish and water plants, or a hedge covered with windblown plastic bags. People often notice these problems and, usually, we can remove them.

Some of the rubbish dumped in the sea washes up on beaches.

Wht Cn U do?

If you see pollution, such as rubbish bags in bushes, tell an adult so that it can be cleaned up and won't harm wildlife.

It's a wonder!

On some beaches, about one-tenth of sand grains are tiny pieces of broken plastic and other rubbish.

↻ Spilled oil from tanker ships into the sea is difficult to clean up, and causes a lot of damage to wildlife.

Waves break apart rubbish into tiny pieces, which mix with the sand on beaches.

Pollution we don't see

Much pollution is unseen. When chemicals are washed into the sea from rivers, they are spread out so we cannot see them and then they damage coral reefs and their creatures. Deep in the forest, animals can cut themselves on broken glass. At sea, turtles that usually feed on jellyfish may eat floating plastic bags.

↪ Pollution affects wildlife. These fish may have been killed by chemicals leaking from a broken factory pipe.

WARNING! Invaders!

In wild places, animals and plants live together in a natural balance. No single kind takes over. When new plants and animals are introduced to an area, it can affect the natural balance.

➲ Removing water weed takes time, money and huge machines.

Introduced water **weeds** spread very fast, carried along by the river currents.

Worst water weed

Sometimes an **introduced species** of plant or animal is brought to a new home, where there is nothing to control it. It becomes a huge pest. Plants can crowd out local flowers and bushes. The water hyacinth is the world's worst water weed. It has spread from South America around the world. It grows so fast that it fills rivers and lakes. Fish die and boats cannot get through it.

Water hyacinth grows so quickly that soon you cannot see the water.

FOCUS ON

Troublesome toads

Cane toads were taken from South America to Australia in the 1930s to eat beetles that were damaging crops. They survived so well that now there are too many of them. They are toxic, so when animals such as snakes and water birds eat them, they die. Local species are now becoming endangered because of this visitor.

Cane toads swarm across roads to find breeding ponds.

On the farm

Introduced farm animals, pets and pests cause massive damage. Sheep and cows eat grass meant for wild grazers. Introduced grey squirrels eat birds' eggs and chicks, and farm dogs upset ground-nesting birds. Local wildlife suffers as it loses its habitat and cannot **breed**. The local balance of nature is badly affected.

In France, farm cows eat grass so that there is little left for other animals.

World famous

Mountain gorillas, Siberian tigers, orang-utans, great whales and Komodo dragons are famously rare. They help us all to be aware of the need to save wildlife.

Why so famous?

Well-known animals are called 'headline species' because they make news headlines. Usually they are fierce, such as lions and eagles, or cuddly, such as giant pandas and tamarin monkeys. Headline species make people think about the dangers facing all wildlife. They encourage us to help, for example, by supporting wildlife charities. If we save their habitats, we also save all the other creatures that live there.

◑ Tagging animals, such as this blue whale in California, USA, helps scientists to learn more about the lives of endangered animals.

Saving wildlife

Scientists are trying to make sure that they can save these headline species. They are researching how the animals live by using **tags**, which allow scientists to watch the animals' movement from a distance. As scientists learn more about their habitats and how these animals live, they hope to help them to survive.

🎧 *There are only about 700 mountain gorillas left in the wild.*

FOCUS ON

Red List

The 'Red List' shows the amount of threat facing rare plants and animals. Those listed as CR, Critically Endangered, are in deepest trouble. Without urgent help, they may be gone in 25 years.

Rhinos are on the Red List.

Tourists and pets

We all like to go on holiday. However, sometimes our holidays affect wildlife. Tropical forests are cut down to build holiday resorts, and wildlife is sold as pets.

◐ People like to watch wildlife. Whale-watching causes little harm as long as people do not get too close.

If beaches are crowded, wildlife may be frightened away.

Holiday fun

Holidays and tourism affect wildlife in different ways. As people take over beaches for sunbathing and swimming, sea turtles who used to lay their eggs in the sand may be frightened away, shellfish are often collected to sell to visitors, and noisy speedboats may scare away fish, dolphins and seals.

Support **ecotourism** if you can. This is when tourists visit places where the local wildlife is respected, cared for and disturbed as little as possible.

Wht Cn U do?

Poor pets

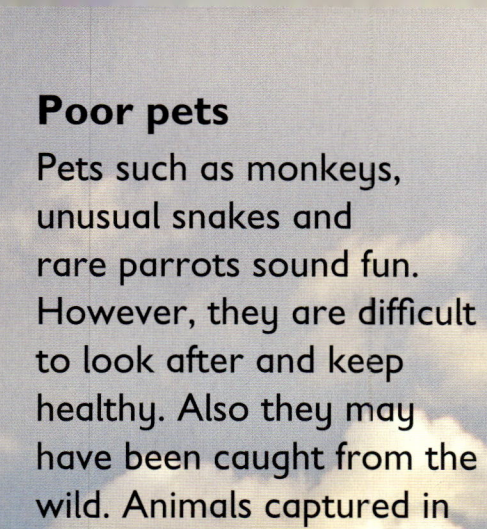

Pets such as monkeys, unusual snakes and rare parrots sound fun. However, they are difficult to look after and keep healthy. Also they may have been caught from the wild. Animals captured in this way suffer in cramped containers without food and water, and many die.

⊂ In some countries, monkeys die in tiny cages while waiting to be sold.

Parrots and macaws are some of the rarest birds in the wild.

⊃ To lay their eggs, sea turtles dig a hole in the sand.

Captive breeding

Some people do not like to see animals in zoos and small wildlife parks. However, for very rare creatures, living in captivity may be the only way to survive.

⊂ Rare animals, such as this baby rhino, are often born and bred in captivity.

⊃ Many wild animals, such as the giant panda, are bred in captivity to be released into the wild.

Last chance

Some animals are so rare and **threatened** that they cannot find partners for breeding, or safe places to live. Keeping them in captivity is their last chance. The captive animals are looked after very carefully. They are studied to find out more about their behaviour and their needs, such as food and shelter. They breed together in captivity to build up their numbers. Then some of them can be **reintroduced** into the wild.

⇧ In zoos, polar bears are given food in ice blocks, so they need to make an effort to feed.

This Californian condor has a tag attached to its wing, so scientists can study it in the wild.

FOCUS ON

Californian condor

The huge birds of prey called Californian condors almost died out. In 1987, only 22 were left. They were captured and bred over several years, and then released. Now there are more than 300. Half of those are already back in the wild.

Back to the wild

There are many captive breeding projects around the world, trying to save a variety of animals such as as red squirrels, wolves, tigers, lizards and rhinos. If there is enough wild space and it is safe for them, they can be released. Animals may be fitted with tags, to follow where they go and see if they survive.

↻ *More than 100 types of monkey are bred in zoos. This helps to increase interest in wildlife.*

Find out if a nearby zoo or wildlife park breeds rare creatures. Perhaps your family or school can hold an event to raise money for them.

SUCCESS stories

Saving wildlife does not stop at keeping an animal in a zoo. It takes lots of time, effort, study, planning – and money.

Tourists can enjoy the beauty of coral reefs with special scuba diving activities.

Protected areas
There are many animals, plants and places saved by the combined efforts of people. Much of Australia's Great Barrier Reef, as well as large areas of tropical forest in Central and South America, Africa and Asia are now protected areas. Visitors can enjoy the wildlife without ruining it.

⊃ When conservation efforts increase tourism, the money made allows facilities, such as water pumps, to be improved.

Wildlife and people

Many people in the world have little food, no clean water or electricity and few comforts. These people need to see the benefits of working to preserve their local wildlife. For example, saving beautiful forests encourages tourists who will bring money into the region. Conservation is not only about saving wildlife, but also protecting people.

It's a wonder!

Black robins have been introduced to different islands, to increase their numbers.

In the 1980s, there were only five black robins of the Chatham Islands, in the Pacific Ocean, left. Now there are more than 250 birds.

HELP us!

Around the world, animals and plants are being saved by fantastic conservation efforts. Wildlife everywhere needs our help.

Many effects

Driving a car can affect polar bears and coral reefs. Burning fuels such as petrol produces greenhouse gases, which are the main cause of global warming. As temperatures rise, icebergs melt and polar bears have fewer places to rest and hunt. Coral reefs become too hot, turn white, or 'bleached', and die. To help save wildlife and habitats, we need to think carefully about what we do each day.

⇨ Planting more trees helps to reduce the greenhouse gas carbon dioxide.

⇦ Using less fuel means less pollution and **climate change**, and saves money!

It's a wonder!

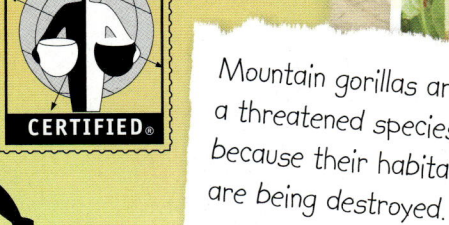

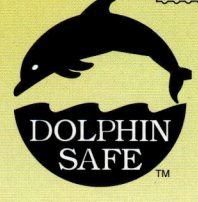

Mountain gorillas are a threatened species because their habitats are being destroyed.

↩ Some products carry a special logo to show that they are friendly to wildlife and the environment.

There are probably more than 25 million kinds, or species, of plant and animal in the world. About half of them live in the habitats most at risk – tropical forests.

⤴ Orang-utans are often killed in the wild by poachers, and their young are left alone.

FOCUS ON

Orang-utans

These apes are becoming rarer every year, as their forests are chopped down for timber and cleared for farmland. They could disappear in your lifetime.

⤴ As forests disappear, male and female orang-utans meet less often to breed.

Too late for some

We may have run out of time to save some animals and plants, and they will sadly become extinct. The Yangtze river dolphin became extinct in 2007. Scientists blame fishing, hunting and shipping for its disappearance.

⤴ The Yangtze river dolphin, or baiji, was last seen alive in 2002.

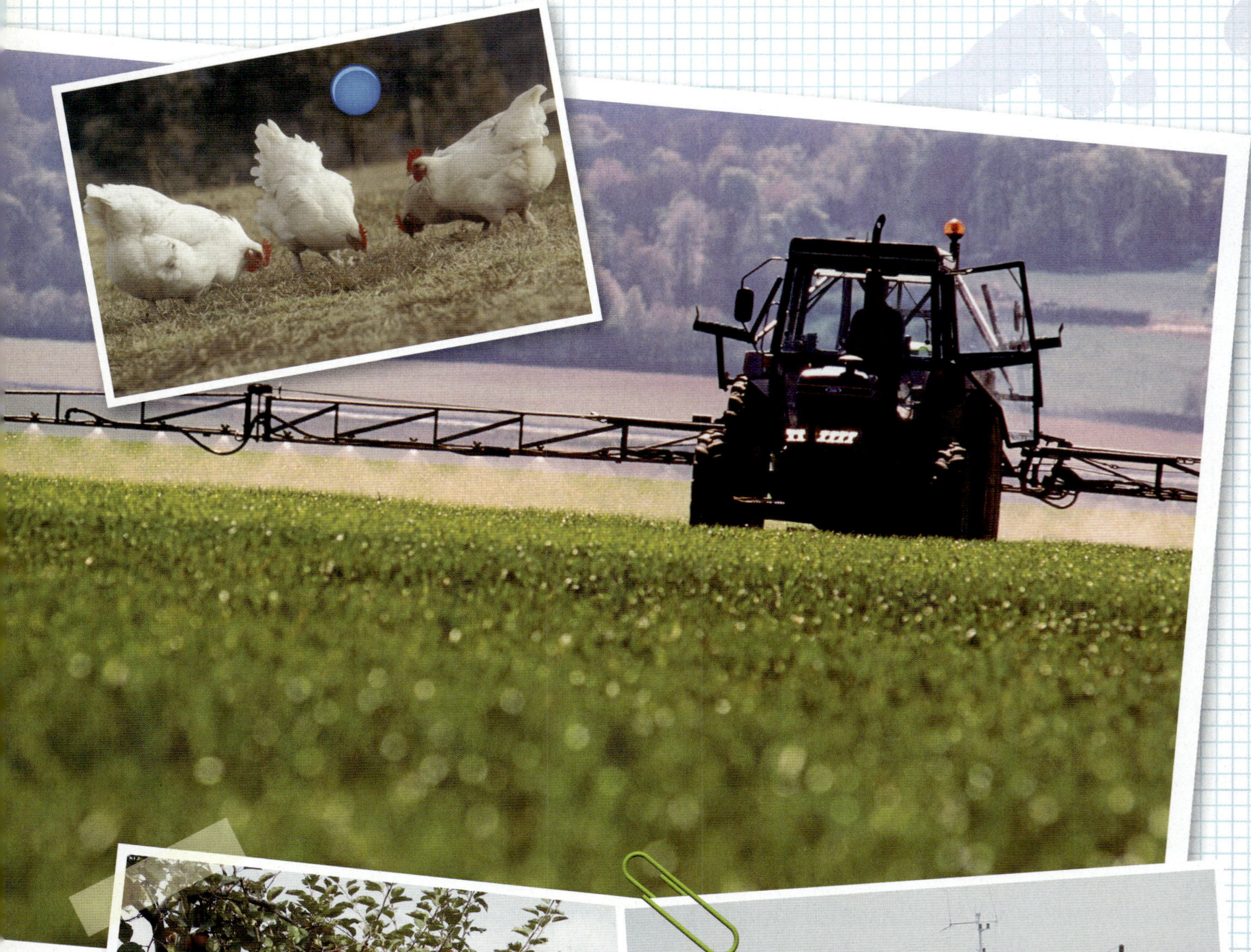
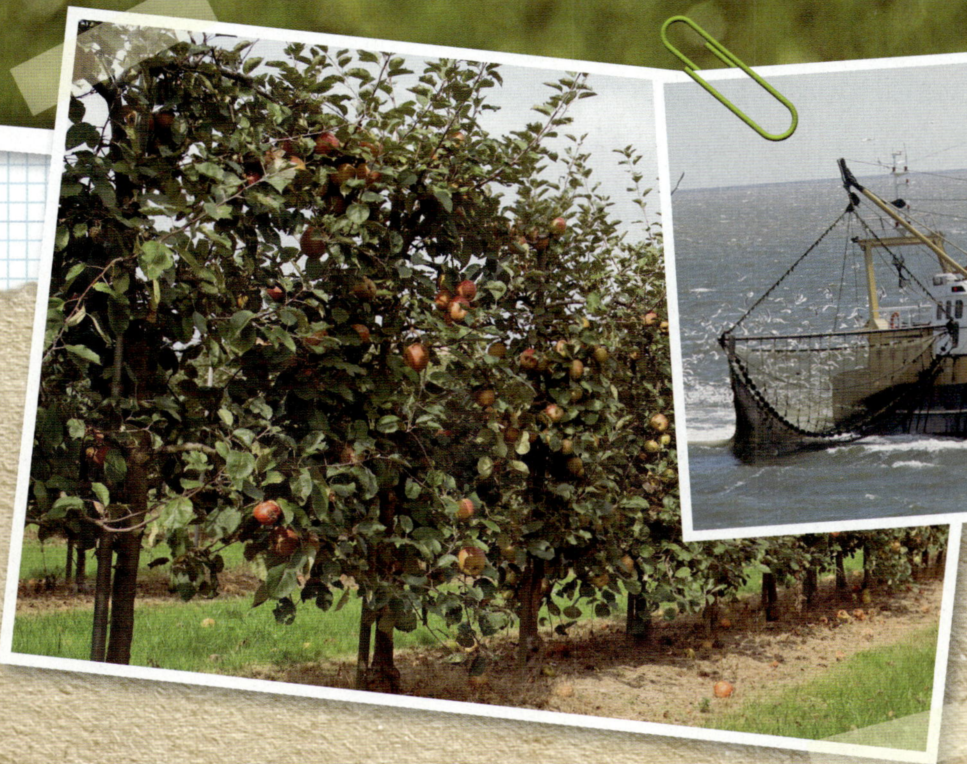
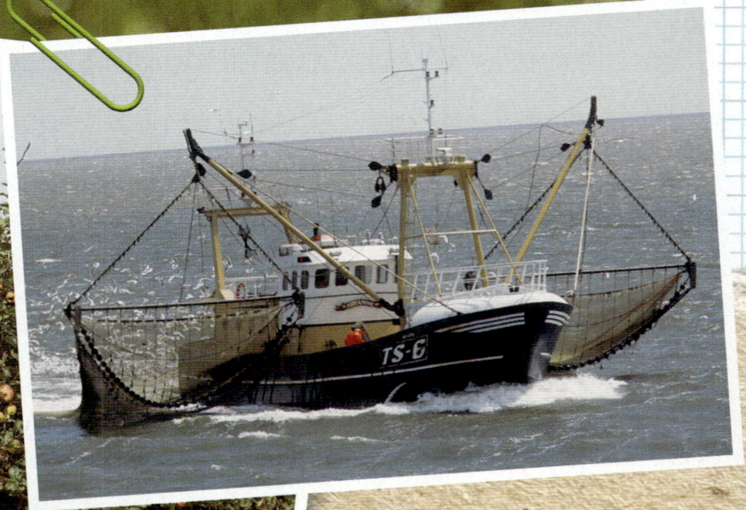

FOOD AND FARMING

As the world's population grows, more food is needed to feed everyone. When land is cleared for farming, habitats are destroyed. Read on to find out how you can help the world by buying local produce and wasting less food.

DOWN ON the farm

Thousands of years ago, there were no farms. People collected wild fruits and other plants, and hunted wild animals to eat. These hunter-gatherers never settled in one place – they moved around the land to find food.

Without machines, early farmers developed pumping systems for water.

↻ Before animals were **domesticated**, people had to plough the land.

A great change

About 15,000 to 12,000 years ago, there was a great change. People began to put wild plant seeds such as wheat, barley, oats and rice in the ground. As the plants grew, the people **harvested**, or gathered, their grains and other products to eat and store. They chose seeds from the best plants to grow the year after, which improved their crops.

Domesticating animals
People also began to keep sheep, goats, pigs and cows, for their milk, meat, fur and skins. Gradually the wild animals became domesticated, or tamed, as **livestock**. As this happened, people began to stay in one place. They built villages and looked after their fields and livestock. They were the first farmers.

Strong cows called oxen ploughed the fields of early farms.

It's a wonder!

Huge machines such as **combine harvesters** do the work of 100 people.

Farming gives us much more food than collecting from the wild. The number of people in the world has gone up from five million about 10,000 years ago to almost 7000 million today.

Growing food

Every minute, nearly 250 babies are born around the world, and so there are more people to feed. As the number of people grows, better farms are needed to produce enough food.

Big business

In some regions, such as the United States of America, farms are more like factories. Growing crops and raising livestock are industries with enormous machines such as tractors, harvesters, helicopters and planes. Farm fields stretch further than you can see. These farms produce much more food than those in poorer regions.

Small farms

In some places of the world, such as in parts of Africa, farms are small. If the weather is bad and crops fail, people may struggle to grow enough to feed themselves. If the weather is good, farmers can grow enough to feed their families and perhaps some extra to sell at market.

◐ This area of farmland in California, USA, is 2000 square kilometres in area. It is divided into squares, like many modern farms, to make the land easier to farm.

In some parts of China, rice is harvested by hand.

In South America, guinea pigs are bred for their meat.

FOCUS ON

Livestock

Many different animals are bred on farms around the world. They are used to work in the fields as well as to supply meat, dairy, wool, fur and leather.

FERTILE land

In some places, farms are very successful and grow lots of crops. In others, the soil is not fertile or the weather is bad, and less food can be produced.

Good for farms

There are good farming conditions across most of Europe, in parts of Asia, and in much of North America, southern South America, New Zealand and eastern Australia. Crops grow well, and there are fields of grassland for livestock.

� In the United States of America, corn is the most highly produced crop. It is mainly used for food and biofuel.

� Fruit orchards thrive with plenty of rich soil, water and sunshine.

Difficult to grow

Some parts of Africa, Asia and South America are too wet for farming. Much of North Africa, the Middle East and central Australia is too dry. All around the far north of the world is covered in ice and snow. It is difficult for people in these places to grow enough food.

It's a wonder!

Good soil is very important for farmers. They need to **preserve** it or crops will fail.

About four-fifths of the world's land is unsuitable for farming. Everyone relies on the remaining one-fifth, so farmers take good care of it.

Farming wood

Farms do not just produce food. They provide many other things that people use every day, such as tea and coffee. Trees are also harvested on farms to produce wood.

So many uses

Wood from trees is used in endless ways, from building houses, sheds and bridges to making beds, tables, chairs and artwork. Trees are also **pulped**, crushed and mixed with water, to make materials such as paper, which we use in books and newspapers.

◉ It can take more than 100 trees to build one timber-frame house.

◉ Pulped trees are used in this factory to produce rolls of paper.

Wood farms

In many places, trees are planted as crops. These places, called timber **plantations**, are wood farms. After many years, the trees are cut down for their wood. Then more trees are planted to replace them. Using wood in this way is **sustainable** – we can grow new supplies so they do not run out. The problem is that some trees are cut down in wild forests and not replaced, and so there are now fewer trees in the world.

It's a wonder!

In the United States, four million trees are planted every day to replace those cut down.

NATURE in danger

Some trees are difficult to farm on plantations as they take hundreds of years to grow. Instead they are cut down from wild places such as tropical rainforests. This damages the homes of wildlife.

Tropical trees

Some of the strongest, most beautiful wood comes from tropical forests, where it is warm all year round. They are known as tropical hardwoods and include teak, mahogany, ebony and rosewood. Products made from these woods are sold for lots of money.

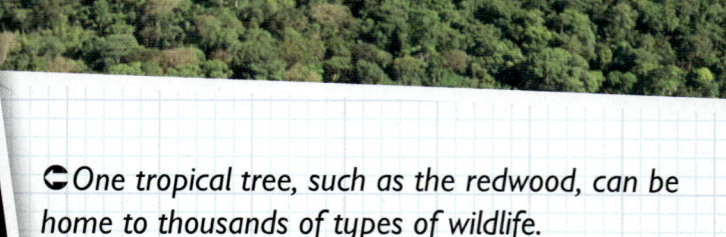

↩ *One tropical tree, such as the redwood, can be home to thousands of types of wildlife.*

What Can U do?

Look at wooden products such as tables, chairs, wardrobes and even spoons. Where does the wood come from? Is it a sustainable supply?

Hotspots

Tropical forests are also '**hotspots**' for wildlife, with very high biodiversity — the variety of animals and plants. As the trees are cut down, animals have nowhere to live and the wildlife disappears. This can lead to **extinction**, as wildlife has nowhere to live and breed.

More than 200 types of monkey, such as this squirrel monkey, are threatened by forest devastation.

⮕ Timber from trees is loaded onto trucks and taken to sawmills.

Double disaster

As tropical forests are cut down for their valuable wood, many other changes happen. The whole natural area, or habitat, may be destroyed.

◑ *This hillside in the Andes, Ecuador, was once covered in trees. The soil is slowly being washed away.*

Washed away

As trees grow upwards, their roots grow down into the soil. The roots help to hold the soil and stop it washing away in the rain. If the trees and their roots are taken away, especially in a rainforest, the heavy rain carries the soil away into the rivers. The land is left bare and no more plants can grow.

◑ *Floods caused by overflowing rivers ruin farm crops and destroy buildings.*

FOCUS ON 📷

Disappearing forests

Tropical forests once covered one-seventh of the world's land. Now they only cover one-seventeenth. Unless we slow the damage, most of them could be gone in 40 years, along with the animals and plants that live there.

Forest is cleared in Brazil for farmers to grow soya crops to sell.

Damaging floods

As the soil washes away, it clogs rivers. The water cannot flow properly and floods the riverbanks, causing damage to surrounding farms and living space.

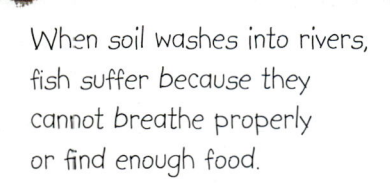

When soil washes into rivers, fish suffer because they cannot breathe properly or find enough food.

Make way for farms

As more farms are needed in the world to produce enough food for people, they take over wild places, and local plants and animals have nowhere to live.

Forest to farm
New farms are often built in cleared forest areas. If the soil washes away, the crops sometimes fail. People then move and clear more wild areas to set up new farms. This causes the damage to quickly spread.

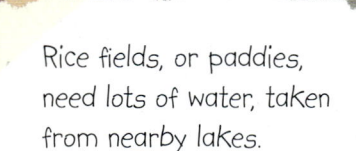

Rice fields, or paddies, need lots of water, taken from nearby lakes.

Wet to dry

Other habitats that are in danger of disappearing are swamps, marshes and other wetlands. Ditches and canals are dug to take away the water to make the soil drier and more suitable for farming. Wetland plants and animals such as frogs, fish, alligators and cranes lose their homes. More than half the world's wetlands have been lost in the past 100 years.

Frogs, such as the African bullfrog, may become endangered in the future if their wetland habitat dries out.

◐ Large birds, such as pelicans, suffer if their water habitats are cleared for farming because they have nowhere to live.

It's a wonder!

On **migration**, many birds must stop over at wetlands.

In 2006, 120 countries in North America, Europe, Africa and West Asia started Wings Over Wetlands, or WOW. They aim to save wetlands where migrating birds stop to rest and feed.

ENDLESS fields

Some farm fields stretch as far as you can see. They grow plenty of food. However, wildlife can suffer as land is taken over for farms.

Is big better?
Large fields mean more crops can be grown. Modern farms have tractors to plough the soil, seed drills for planting and harvesters to gather crops. These machines are large and need space, so farmers cut down hedges and trees that get in their way. Fewer trees and hedges mean animals have nowhere to shelter.

Combine harvesters can clear a huge field in a few hours.

Chemical sprays
Some farmers spray their crops to protect them from pests that eat the crops. The chemical sprays not only kill pests, but they can also harm animals such as butterflies and birds. The chemicals spread to the soil and water, causing pollution.

Wind may blow farm sprays to nearby natural areas such as woods, killing other plants and animals.

Good farming

Farmers can change the crop in a field every year. This is called crop rotation. It keeps the soil healthy and reduces pests. Planting hedges gives shelter to birds and other creatures that eat the pests on crops.

Fields are ploughed to turn over the top layer of the soil, bringing fresh nutrients to the surface.

◒ By growing different crops, different nutrients are added to the soil.

ALL ORGANIC PRODUCE

◒ Organic food may taste better than food grown with chemicals and sprays.

Wht Cn U do?

'Organic' vegetables and fruits are grown in ways that are good for wildlife and the soil. Have a look in your local store or supermarket for organic labels.

Hi-tech farming

On farms, cows, pigs and chickens used to wander freely in the fields. Now, farmers need to change the way animals are kept because we need more food and therefore more space, which we don't have.

Indoor animals

On many modern farms, animals are kept indoors. A smaller space is used compared to an outside area, and more food, such as meat and eggs, can be produced. Cows and pigs live in big barns and chickens stay in sheds. They are kept warm and fed specially made food.

New crops

Scientists can alter farm crops by changing the genes – tiny chemical 'instructions' inside them that control how they grow. This is called **genetic modification**, or GM. GM crops may be able to grow in poor soil and not be destroyed by pests, so more food is produced.

Genetically modified cotton can also be grown. This gives farmers a better crop to sell.

'Free-range' farm animals can wander in yards or fields, rather than being kept indoors. Look for 'free-range' labels on eggs, chicken, pork and other meat products.

Wht Cn U do?

◐ Instead of being kept in fields, cows sometimes live in barns.

Free-range chickens roam freely outside.

79

Farming the sea

Farms are not just on land. They are in water, too. Many kinds of fish are farmed for us to eat. They can be taken from the sea or special fish farms.

Fishing fleets

Many kinds of wild fish are caught in the oceans, such as sardines, tuna, cod and salmon, and shellfish such as mussels, crabs and prawns. Modern fishing boats are so big and effective that in some areas they have caught too many fish. There are none left to breed. This is known as **overfishing**. It will take many years for fish numbers to become high again.

◐ In some areas, overfishing has meant there are hardly any fish for boats to catch.

Captive fish

Wild fish can also be farmed in huge tanks on land, and in giant cages floating in the sea. The fish are well fed, grow fast and are easy to catch. Sometimes they may suffer diseases from being too crowded.

⊃ *Salmon are raised in massive cages in lakes and along coasts.*

📷 FOCUS ON

Bycatch

Dolphins, seals and other animals are sometimes caught accidentally as 'bycatch' in fishing nets. This has helped to cause some species, such as sea turtles, to become endangered.

Some species of sea turtles are endangered because large numbers of them die when they get caught in nets.

Energy farms

Some farm crops are grown as a source of energy. They are burned for heating and cooking, as fuels in vehicles, and in power stations to make electricity. They are known as biofuels.

▶ Corn is one of the most widely grown crops in the world. A lot of it is grown in the USA and China.

Biofuels

Some biofuels come from plants with oily seeds, such as palm, sunflower, soya and canola (rapeseed). The seeds are squeezed or pressed to remove the oil, which is treated with chemicals and burned, for example, as biodiesel. Other biofuels such as sugar cane are left to ferment, or rot. They produce gases such as methane or liquids such as ethanol, which are burned to produce energy.

Cooking oil is made into biofuel in large machines in factories.

Sustainable fuels

We use a lot of fossil fuels — coal, oil and gas — and they are running out. Biofuels are sustainable — we can replace them by growing new crops every year. Biofuel plants such as sugar cane also take in the greenhouse gas carbon dioxide as they grow, which helps to reduce global warming.

A vehicle needs to be changed to work with biofuel, which can be bought at some filling stations.

These soya bean fields in Brazil were once tropical rainforest.

FOCUS ON

Biofuel problems

Biofuel crops may be grown on land that was once a natural habitat, meaning wildlife has been destroyed or lost its home. Or they can be grown on land once used for food crops, so local people cannot farm.

Mountains and miles

Some places have successful farms and grow too much food. Other places don't have enough food. This is because of different farming conditions.

Too much food

Successful farmers have 'food mountains' of produce such as wheat and potatoes. The farmer has to pay huge costs to store these foods properly, keep them free of pests and disease, and transport them to faraway places where people lack food. Sometimes the spare food ends up being ploughed back into the soil.

Giant grain tanks are used to store crops until they are sold.

◐ If food is not sold, sometimes it is left to rot.

Moving animals over long distances costs money. This adds to the price of meat.

World travel

In a big food store, you can buy all kinds of fruit, vegetable, spices, meat and other food from around the world. Transporting these by ship, plane, train and truck uses up fuel energy and other resources. It adds to problems of pollution and global warming. Foods grown locally mean fewer 'food miles' and fewer problems for the natural world.

Wht Cn U do?
Look at fruit, vegetable and meat labels in a supermarket to see where they come from. Visit a local farmers' market, where the foods are usually grown nearby and stored for less time. It is better to choose foods that do not travel far.

◀ Local market produce is often sold shortly after it has been harvested.

Keeping shelves full

Millions of people around the world are starving, and suffering from diseases caused by lack of food and clean water. As the number of people increases, these problems may get worse.

Enough for everyone
The world's farmers can produce enough food to feed everyone, but this food isn't shared equally around the world. The main problem is that many people do not have enough land to grow food, or enough money to buy it.

↑ *Stocks of food aid are piled up to be sent to the village of Yama in northwestern Niger.*

Climate and farming

Global warming is caused mainly by carbon dioxide gas, which is produced by burning fossil fuels. It will alter the weather and cause climate change. This could cause farming areas to suffer floods, droughts, storms and other problems. Also some kinds of farming use lots of machinery, energy, materials and other resources, which is not sustainable. More natural ways of farming help to reduce these problems.

When farmland is flooded, crops are usually ruined. This costs the farmer money.

It's a wonder!

In 1992, the number of very hungry people in the world was about 850 million. In 2002, it had gone down to 820 million.

Refugees line up in Darfur, Africa, to receive food aid donated by other countries.

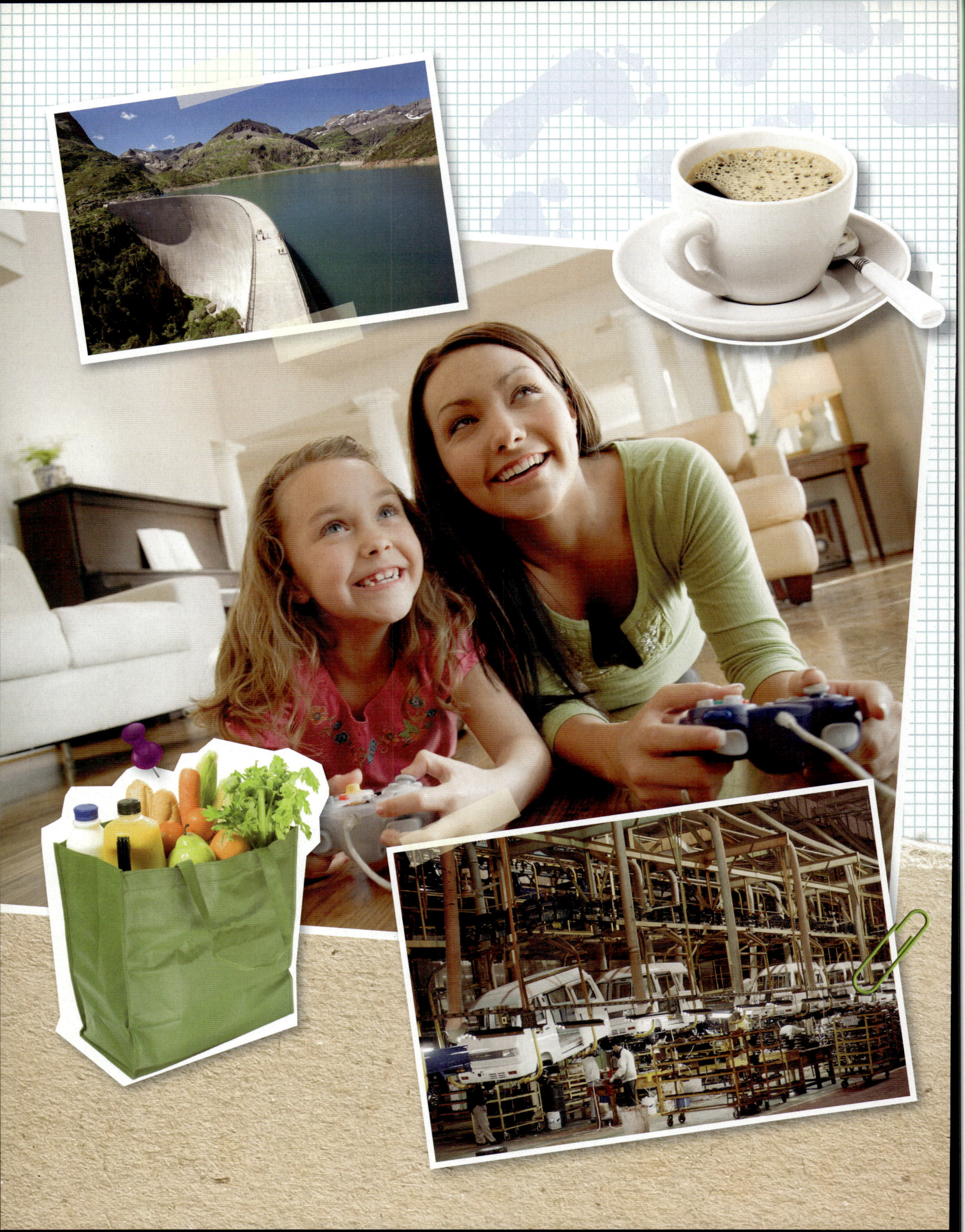

POPULATION

The population of the world is increasing. This puts pressure on the Earth because of the extra people that need places to live, as well as food and water. Read on to find out how your efforts can make a difference.

Only one world

The planet we live on, Earth, provides us with everything we need to live – space to build our homes, food to eat and air to breathe.

◊ Cities not only use vast amounts of materials and energy – they produce huge quantities of waste.

Our planet

Planet Earth provides all our needs and resources. Its vital substances, such as air, food and water, keep us alive. It also provides the raw materials to make our homes and buildings, and our machines and gadgets, from jumbo jets to cars.

It's a wonder!

One world isn't enough for the way we live now. We are using up the resources too fast.

Around the world, we need 1.3 planets to provide the resources we need and absorb the waste we produce. This means that it takes Earth one year and four months to renew what we use in one year.

Running out

Every day, we are using up Earth's raw materials, energy and other resources. The planet may seem big enough for these supplies to last for ever, but they won't. The way we live today is not sustainable, which means it cannot last forever.

Pollution from factories and power stations spreads around the world.

Footprints

A 'footprint' describes the effect our lifestyle has on Earth. We are constantly putting pressure on the planet to supply our needs.

Eco-print

An **ecological** footprint measures how much space you need to survive. It includes where your share of food, water, fuel and other resources comes from, and even where your rubbish goes to. Everyone has a different ecological footprint, and it is important for us all to know how big an impact we are having on the Earth.

⬆ Factories use a lot of energy when they make products, such as plastic.

A mobile phone needs materials to produce it and energy to make it work.

C-print

Burning fuels such as coal, oil, gas and wood produces the gas carbon dioxide. This is causing global warming. A **carbon footprint** is the amount of carbon dioxide and similar gases that we produce. It measures the effect human activity has on the planet.

Big metal tanks store natural gas fuel from deep underground.

Don't leave appliances on standby – it's better to turn them off. In the UK, two power stations' worth of electricity are wasted each year because television sets and other gadgets are left on standby. This costs 740 million pounds a year!

FOCUS ON

Global footprint

The combination of all the footprints is called a **global footprint**. It shows the overall pressure we put on the Earth.

Making small changes, such as using low-energy light bulbs, can add up to big energy savings.

Plenty of people

The population of the world is increasing. About five babies are born and two people die every second. That's 120 extra people on Earth a minute!

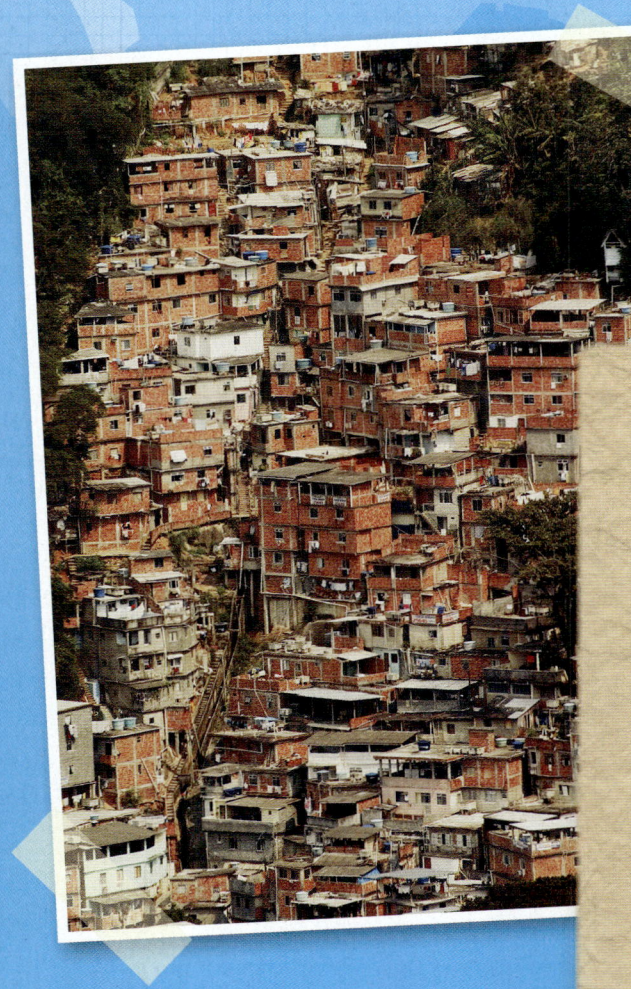

More pressure
These extra people need somewhere to live, and basic supplies such as food and water. Every minute, more strain is put on the Earth and its resources.

It's a wonder!
Population is the number of people living in a certain area. Some countries have more people than others. In an area the size of Wembley football pitch, the number of people these countries have is...

- SINGAPORE has 60
- UK has 2.5
- USA has 0.3
- AUSTRALIA has 0.025

⇧ City houses pack closely together in some areas of Rio de Janeiro, Brazil.

When a lot of people live in one area, it becomes very crowded.

Country to city

In some parts of the world, such as deserts, you can walk all day and see no one. In other places, such as cities, you can hardly move for crowds of people.

A desert is an extreme habitat. People who live there may use camels to travel around.

Pressure for space

For hundreds of years people have been moving from the countryside to towns and cities. In 2007, for the first time, more people lived in cities than in villages. The problem is that city people do not grow their own food and spreading cities mean there is less land for farms. This puts extra pressure on our planet to provide food and new places to grow it.

➲ *The population of the world is rising faster. It is thought that by 2050, it will reach nine billion people.*

Population of the world: AD 0–2050

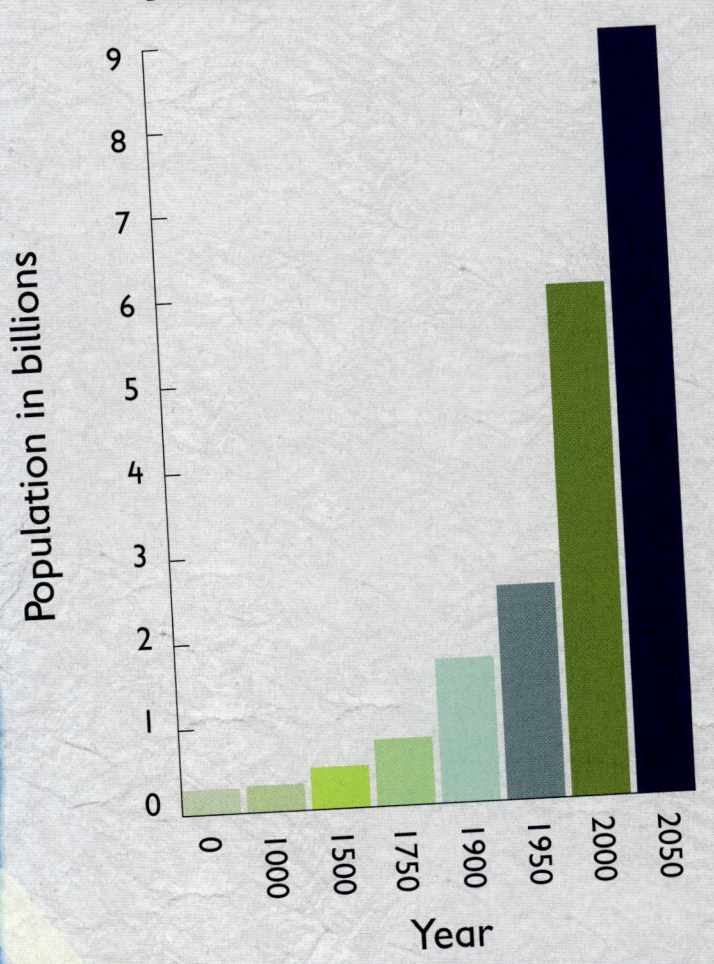

RAW materials

In order to make products that we use every day, such as cars and computers, we use the Earth's natural resources, such as oil.

Raw materials
To make products, factories and industries need raw materials from the Earth. Many products have parts made from plastics. These plastics come from the raw material oil, or petroleum, which is found in oil wells drilled deep below the Earth's surface.

↻ *Huge rigs drill down thousands of metres into the seabed to reach oil underground.*

Supply of materials

Finding raw materials means drilling, mining and quarrying. This uses up energy, affects huge areas of land and produces pollution. The supplies of raw materials will run out one day.

⮕ When vehicles are made in factories, raw materials and a large amount of energy are used.

Metals

Industry uses metal – for example, **aluminium** for drinks cans and aircraft, **steel** in cars and **copper** in electrical wires. Metals occur in rocks, called **ores**. The rocks are dug from mines and **quarries**. Then they are crushed and heated or treated to extract, or get out, the pure metal.

Half of the copper produced in the world comes from the ore, Chalcopyrite.

Look for 'green' labels on products. These show if they have been made carefully, using the least raw materials and energy, and do little damage to the environment.

Energy to burn

Almost everything we make and do needs energy, from warming our homes to mending roads. Most of this energy comes from burning fuels.

◐ Leigh Creek is a coal-mining town in Australia. About 2.5 million tonnes of coal is dug here every year.

Fossil fuels

The main fuels are oil, coal and natural gas. They are called fossil fuels because they are preserved, or fossilized, remains of living things from millions of years ago. They are burned in power stations to make electricity, and in homes and buildings for heating. Oil is the raw material for the petrol and diesel that is burned in vehicles. We cannot replace fossil fuels and they are running out fast.

Alternative fuels

Non-fossil **alternative fuels** include wood and biofuels from plants. They are sustainable — we can grow new supplies so they do not run out.

FOCUS ON

How much is left?

At today's rates of use, how much fossil fuel is left?
- Oil - less than 100 years
- Natural gas - less than 150 years
- Coal - less than 200 years

⬅ Natural gas has to be treated at a processing plant to take away the unwanted parts. This is then safe for us to use.

It's a wonder!

Passenger planes such as jumbo jets use a lot of fuel. In just 15 seconds, one jumbo jet burns the same amount of fuel as in one car's full tank.

Warmer world

Burning fuels emits, or produces, the gas carbon dioxide. This is a greenhouse gas that soaks up the Sun's heat. Burning more fuels means more carbon emissions, which causes the Earth to get hotter. This is called global warming.

Climate change
Global warming is changing our weather and climate. This is called climate change. Most places are getting warmer, but some areas may become cooler. Wet places could dry out, and dry areas could become wetter. There will probably be more hurricanes, floods and other extreme weather.

◐ Bangladesh is a country that has been badly affected by flooding. These farm fields along the Jamuna River are underwater, ruining the crops.

Importance of carbon

The carbon footprint makes up more than half of our overall global footprint. It's produced by our lifestyle – how much electricity and petrol we use, when we make goods, grow food and use transport.

⊂ **Solar panels** use the Sun to make electricity.

Water flowing through pipes in a hydroelectric dam creates electricity.

FOCUS ON

Sustainable electricity

Electricity can be made from sources of energy that do not produce carbon dioxide. These include water (hydroelectricity), wind, tides and **geothermal energy** deep in the ground.

GOING places

People in some countries can go where they want, when they want, in their cars. This adds greatly to our global footprint.

In a traffic jam, many cars are burning fuel, even though they are not moving.

The main villain
Cars take huge amounts of raw materials and energy to make. Running them burns fossil fuels, which causes pollution and carbon emissions. Traffic jams make this many times worse.

Green transport

'Green' transport produces less carbon, less pollution and less noise, and is more sustainable. It includes electric vehicles and hybrid cars with a combination of a petrol engine and electric motor. Cycling and walking are the greenest because they produce no pollution.

◐ *Hybrid cars are powered by both electricity and fuel. They use less fuel and produce less carbon dioxide, making them better for the planet.*

Helping the C-print

Public transport includes buses, coaches and trains. Their overall carbon emissions are far less than private cars. Some cities have park-and-ride systems where you drive to a car park nearby, then use public transport into the centre. This produces fewer carbon emissions.

📷 FOCUS ON

Carbon emissions

How do carbon emissions compare for a typical journey?

- Trains and coaches produce the least. The more people in them, the better it is for the carbon footprint!

- Cars and planes produce two to ten times more, especially if travelling long distances.

◑ *More buses mean fewer traffic jams, so everyone travels faster.*

House and home

Every day, as we heat our homes, take hot showers, play computer games and watch television – we add to our carbon footprint.

Daily life

People need to stay warm, keep clean, eat and do fun activities. The key is to take care in daily life. For example, heating uses huge amounts of energy. We can reduce the effect on the environment by switching off heating and lights when a room isn't being used.

It's a wonder!

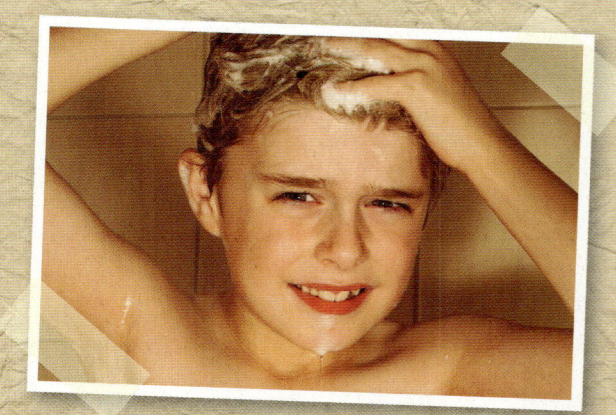

A quick shower uses five times less water and heat than a bath, and gets you cleaner!

Too many gadgets

Many people use computers, mp3 players and other electric gadgets. Each one has a footprint – the raw materials, energy, industrial equipment and carbon emissions needed to make it.

⌃All of these gadgets need electricity to work. They should always be turned off when they are not being used.

Find out how your home stops warmth from escaping. Does it have an insulated roof and walls, double-glazed windows and well-fitting doors? All this helps to save heat and reduce your footprint – and save money!

Wht Cn U do?

Watch that waste!

Raw materials, energy and machinery are needed to make the products we use every day. If we throw things away, this creates a lot of waste. That's why the four 'Rs' are so important.

Reduce

We can reduce waste by using less. Reduce the need for new plastic shopping bags by taking your own re-usable bags. Buy items loose rather than in containers. Avoid buying things with huge amounts of packaging.

A material bag that can be reused is better than using new plastic bags each time you go shopping.

Repair

If something is broken, instead of throwing it away, try to get it repaired. Broken televisions and computers can often be fixed, and ripped clothing can be mended.

You can mend and alter clothes, and make new ones by learning to sew.

Re-use

Re-use items in new ways. Jars can be washed and re-used as containers. Magazines and greetings cards can be re-used to make pieces of art.

Recycle

Recycling is making new products from used materials. Glass, metals, paper, card and most plastics can all be recycled. Making a bottle from recycled glass uses only one-tenth of the energy needed for a brand-new bottle.

- Recycle as much as you can. For example, use a compost bin for vegetable scraps and garden waste.
- Rainwater can then be used for the garden, and washing cars and bicycles.

⇒ Rainwater can be collected in a water butt. It is free and clean.

⇐ Before paper and card are recycled, they go through a sorting machine to separate them.

FOOD and health

Food does not appear by magic in supermarkets and shops. It is grown, cleaned, stored, transported and processed into ready-made meals or snacks. All this is an important part of our global footprint.

Old and new

Many years ago, most people grew their own food plants and kept animals such as chickens, sheep or cows. Today food is big business, with expensive machines used for planting, harvesting and cleaning crops, planes for transporting crops, enormous cold stores, and factories for processing. Making and running all these machines adds to our global footprint.

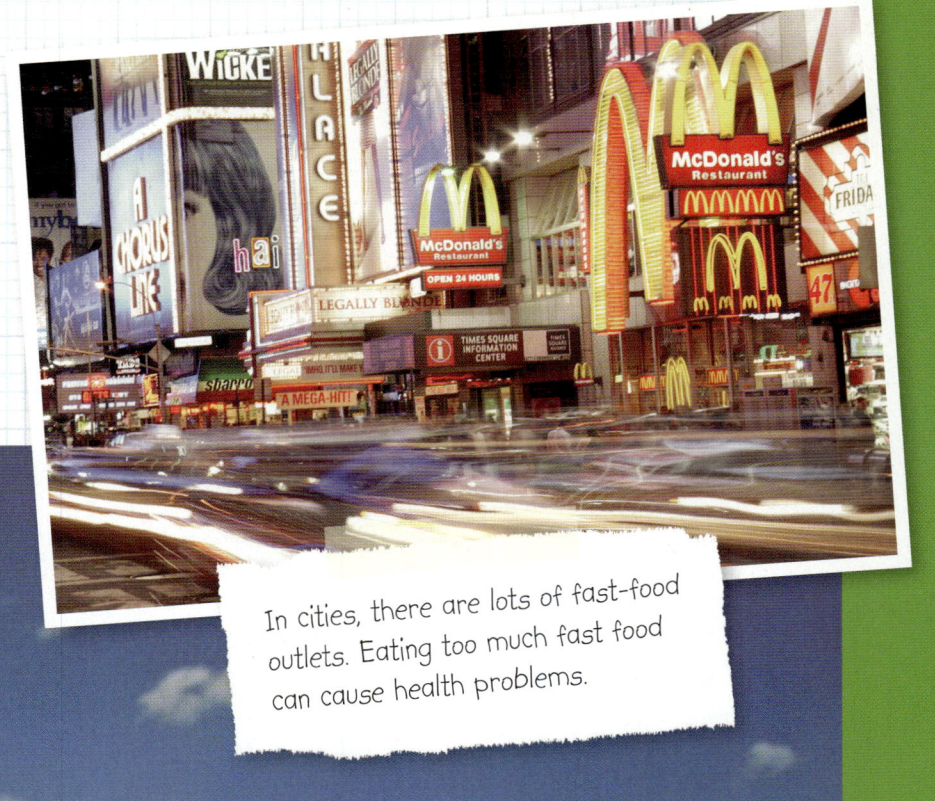

Health problems

In some countries, there is not enough food for everyone. This can cause starvation, which brings illness and disease. In other countries, there is a lot of food available, so people may eat too much. This can also cause health problems, such as obesity and heart disease.

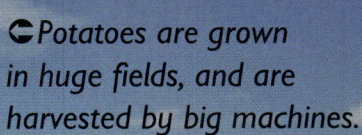

In cities, there are lots of fast-food outlets. Eating too much fast food can cause health problems.

◐ Potatoes are grown in huge fields, and are harvested by big machines.

📷 FOCUS ON

Food waste

In countries such as the UK or USA, each year an average person throws away enough food to feed someone for two weeks. This is a waste of all the resources used to grow and prepare that food.

In the UK, eight billion pounds worth of food is thrown away every year – that's a third of everything bought.

Losing wild places

As we take over land for towns, cities, factories, farms, mines and quarries, wild places shrink. This leaves less land for plants and animals to live on.

Rare animals

Most people know about rare animals such as tigers, mountain gorillas, giant pandas and great whales. These are just a few of the thousands of threatened creatures and plants around the world. Their main problem is habitat destruction – when we damage or take over their natural places for our own needs. Other threats include pollution, hunting and fishing, as well as global warming and climate change.

⮕ *Scientists can watch endangered species, such as the oribi, by fitting them with a radio collar.*

Wht Cn U do?
- Support wildlife projects and charities.
- Join an organized clean-up of a local wood, lake, beach or other habitat.

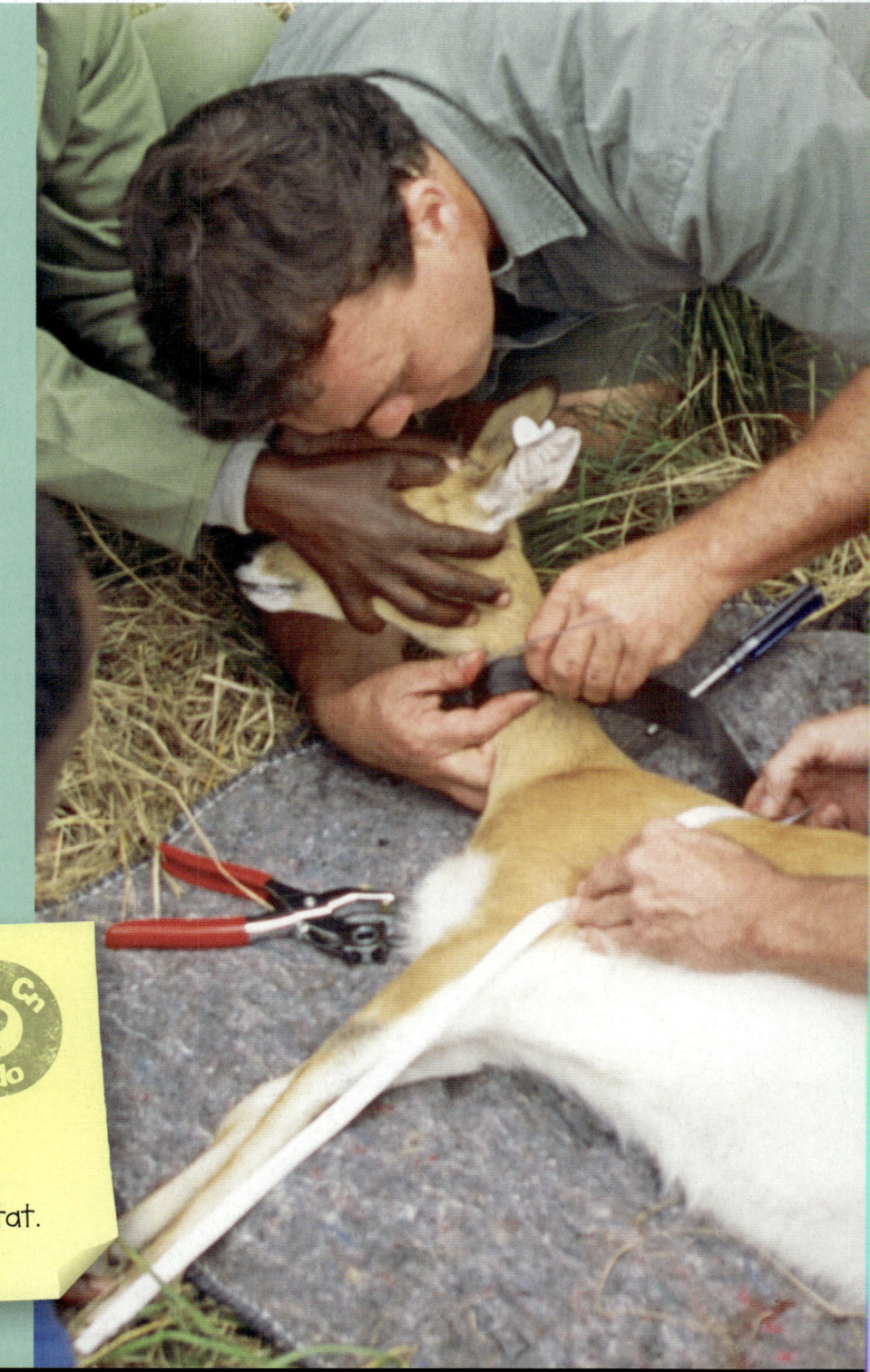

Conservation

We can help wildlife in many ways, and reduce our global footprint, too. Protected places such as nature reserves and national parks are vital. We can clean up damaged areas and return them to nature. Rare animals are saved by being bred in captivity, then being released into the wild.

The African wild ass is bred in zoos and nature reserves because it has become endangered.

Red spotted newts need clean water, but their streams and rivers are becoming polluted.

It's a wonder!

There are more than 6000 kinds of frog, toad, newt, salamander and other amphibian – and about one-third are under threat.

Fairtrade

The food we buy in supermarkets and the clothes we wear are often produced by workers in other parts of the world. We need to make sure that these workers are paid fairly for producing goods for us.

Hard work, low pay

Clothes, food and toys in our shops are sometimes produced in faraway countries. Workers may be children, may not be paid very much, and have to work long hours in cramped conditions. These products are often sold to companies that then sell them to us.

In some countries, children are expected to work. These children are weaving carpets in factories.

← Clean, well-lit conditions and suitable clothes are very important at work. These workers are in a toy factory in China.

↻ Coffee beans are hand-picked from bushes, then sold to companies that make them into the drink.

More equal

'Fairtrade' tries to make sure that workers have a safe and healthy place to work, and that they are paid fairly for the goods they produce. It also helps people who buy the goods to realize that they can be made with fewer materials and less waste. Fairtrade is a way of helping workers earn a good living, in a healthy environment.

Wht Cn U do?
- Look for 'fairtrade' labels on products.
- Where are they made?
- How do their prices compare with other similar products?

↑ The fairtrade label shows that the product has been made in a fair way.

Bananas that have been grown by fairtrade farmers have a special sticker.

Be aware!

Almost everything we do adds to our global footprint. To save the Earth, we all need to take action. Even small efforts, such as turning off an unused light, reduce the pressure put on the Earth.

Need to know

We need to learn about global footprints, fossil fuels and climate change so that we can change our lifestyle. Education to increase people's awareness is very important. If people see an advertisement on television about recycling, they may start to recycle more, to help our planet and our future.

FOCUS ON

WWF's Earth hour

On 28 March at 8.30 p.m. hundreds of millions of people across 4000 cities and towns switched off their lights for one hour. Iconic buildings took part, too, including...

The Empire State Building
Big Ben
Sydney Opera House
The Eiffel Tower
The Pyramids of Giza
Bird's Nest Stadium

Rising powers

Countries such as China, India and Brazil are developing industries at amazing rates. Their global footprints are rising. But they are still not as high as those of people in the USA and UK. Every country needs to be aware of what they can do to reduce the effect of their lifestyle on the planet, and start changing their footprint to make a difference.

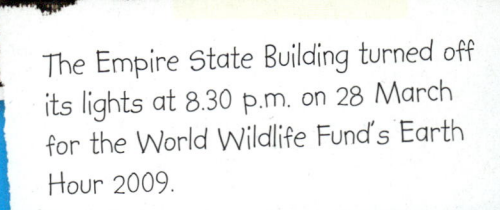

The Empire State Building turned off its lights at 8.30 p.m. on 28 March for the World Wildlife Fund's Earth Hour 2009.

◔ Shanghai, in China, now has more than 20 million people and is the world's busiest port for ships and boats.

Glossary

Adapt To change to suit the surroundings better. For example, when a living thing develops features that help it to survive in a particular place or environment.

Alternative energy Energy that is produced in ways that do not damage or pollute the environment. Alternative energy cannot run out.

Alternative fuels Non-fossil fuels (not coal, oil or natural gas) that are sustainable and cause little damage to our surroundings, such as wood.

Aluminium A lightweight metal that does not rust. It is used for many purposes such as making drinks cans.

Biodiversity The variety of different living things found in one habitat.

Biofuels Fuels that come from living things such as crops, and provide energy when they are burnt.

Breed To reproduce or make more of a species.

Bycatch When fish or other water animals are caught accidentally, usually by being trapped in nets, and are not the creatures intended to be caught.

Captivity When animals are contained and cared for by humans, such as in a zoo or wildlife park.

Carbon dioxide A gas that is naturally present in tiny amounts in air. It is produced by burning, and acts as a powerful greenhouse gas.

Carbon emissions The emission, or giving off, of gases that contain carbon, especially carbon dioxide.

Carbon footprint The amount of carbon dioxide and similar gases produced to supply a person's lifestyle, including food, a place to live and transport.

Chemical In crop sprays, a substance that is used to kill certain living things, such as weeds, moulds or insect pests.

Climate The average pattern of temperature, rainfall, winds and other weather conditions in a particular place over hundreds or thousands of years.

Climate change Changes in the long-term weather patterns around the world due to global warming, including more extreme weather such as storms, floods and droughts.

Combine harvester A farming machine that combines several harvesting jobs, such as cutting a crop and separating the wanted parts – seeds – from the unwanted parts – stems.

Conserve To save living things and the natural habitats or places where they live, by protecting them against damage by people, pollution and other problems.

Copper A soft reddish-brown metal that allows electricity and heat to pass through it easily.

Coral reef A rocky area in shallow, warm seawater, providing a habitat for many different living things.

Crops Plants grown and harvested (gathered) by people for many purposes, such as rice, wheat and potatoes for food, or straw for making thatched roofs, or sugar cane to make biofuel.

Desert A very dry place that has little or no rain.

Disease An illness or sickness that causes problems in the body, makes people feel unwell and may cause death.

Domesticated Plants and animals that are mostly tame. They are used to farm crops and as pets.

Drought An unusually long period of time without rain.

Ecological To do with ecology, which is the scientific study of how plants and animals live together in their surroundings or environment.

Ecotourism Tourism (visiting places on holiday) that has the least effect on the local plants, animals and habitats. It also raises money to conserve habitats and their wildlife.

Endangered When a type of living thing is under threat or at risk of extinction.

Equator An imaginary band around the middle of the Earth, halfway between the North and South Pole.

Extinct Describes a type of animal or plant that has died out completely so that there is none left anywhere in the world.

Extinction When a type of animal or plant has died out completely so that there is none left anywhere in the world.

Fertile In farming, soil that has plenty of nutrients and goodness, so that crops grow well in it.

Flood Too much water in a place that usually has little or no water.

Fossil Any part of a dead plant or animal that has been preserved in rock.

Fossil fuels Fuels made from the remains of once-living things that died long ago, were buried and preserved in the rocks. The main fossil fuels are oil (petroleum), natural gas and coal.

Genetic modification, GM Altering the natural genes or chemical 'instructions' inside a living thing, such as adding a gene to make it grow faster.

Geothermal energy Heat energy from deep in the ground, where the rocks get hotter as you go deeper.

Global footprint A combination of carbon footprint, ecological footprint and other footprints. It shows the overall pressure that people's lifestyles put on Earth.

Global warming The rise in the temperature of the atmosphere. It is caused by increased amounts of greenhouse gases, which are produced when burning fuels.

Grassland A habitat such as the North American prairies or African savanna, where the main plants are grasses, rather than trees, bushes or other plants.

Greenhouse gas A gas that helps to take in the Sun's heat and make the atmosphere around Earth warmer.

Habitat A kind of place where animals and plants live, such as a river, wood, desert or coral reef.

Harvest To gather or collect plant parts such as fruits, especially for food, and also for other uses, such as harvesting reeds to make thatch for roofs.

Heatwave An unusually long period of high temperatures.

Hotspot A popular place.

Hurricane A large powerful storm with fast winds that swirl round and lots of heavy rain.

Hydroelectricity Electricity that is made using moving water.

Introduced species Types of plants and animals that are taken from where they are found naturally to new places where they did not live before.

Livestock Farm animals that are domesticated (tamed) and are kept for their meat, fur or hair, skins, milk and pulling power.

Manmade chemicals Substances made by humans that may have harmful effects. For example, chemical sprays for farm crops that kill weeds or pests.

Methane A gas made when things rot or when animals digest food.

Migration When birds or other animals travel regularly from one part of the world to another.

Nature reserve A place that is protected or set aside for wildlife to live freely, without being threatened by people.

Nuclear power Electricity that is made by splitting or breaking apart the centres of atoms.

Ore A rock that contains metal.

Organic In farming, crops and livestock that are raised in a mainly natural way, without artificial chemicals such as pesticides and fertilizers.

Overfishing Catching too many fish or other water animals from an area, so there are not enough left to breed and carry on their kind.

Oxygen A gas that makes up one-fifth of the air around us. Humans and animals breathe oxygen to stay alive.

Plantations Areas planted by people with the same kind of crop, usually a type of tree, such as oil palm trees for palm oil, or spruce trees for timber (wood).

Plough To turn over the soil by pulling along a large curved metal blade before planting seeds.

Polar The region around the North Pole or the South Pole, at the top or bottom of the Earth, where it is cold all year round.

Pollution When harmful substances such as chemicals or litter get into the surroundings and cause damage.

Power station A building that has machines called generators to make electricity.

Predator An animal that hunts and kills other creatures, called prey, to eat as food.

Preserve To save something from being destroyed or harmed.

Pulp To crush something until it almost becomes a liquid.

Quarry A place where rocks are dug out of the ground.

Radioactive Giving off harmful rays, called radiation, that can cause serious illness, burns and even death.

Rainforest A forest where it rains on most days throughout the year.

Rare When there are very few of a particular plant or animal.

Reintroduce To breed a type of animal or plant in captivity and then put it back into a suitable wild place, hopefully to live freely and survive.

Smog Polluted air that looks like a mixture of smoke and fog. It is caused by burning fuels in cars and factories.

Solar panels Special panels that use the heat and light of the Sun to create solar energy.

Species A type of plant or animal where the individuals look similar and breed together to produce young.

Steel A hard, strong metal that contains mainly iron and small amounts of carbon.

Sustainable Something that can carry on for a very long time, without running out or wearing away.

Tag A small label or radio device that is harmlessly attached to an animal, so that it can be identified and its movements followed.

Temperate Not too hot or too cold.

Threaten To put at risk or in danger. A threatened species is at risk of becoming extinct.

Tropical The region around the middle of the Earth, on either side of the Equator, where it is warm all year.

Tropical forest A large area of trees growing near the Equator, where it is warm all year round. These forests are the richest and most varied places in the world for wildlife.

Water vapour Water in the form of a gas, which is invisible and floats in the air.

Weather Conditions such as the temperature, amount of rain and wind strength, and how these conditions change from day to day and week to week.

Weed A plant that grows where we do not want it to grow.

Index

adaptation 39
African bullfrogs 75
African wild asses 111
Aral Sea 25
atmosphere 10, 11, 23, 27, 28, 29

beavers 42
biodiversity 41, 71
biofuels 31, 66, 82–83, 99
black robins 57
brine shrimps 39
bushmeat 45
bycatch 81

cactus plants 38
Californian condors 55
cane toads 49
captive breeding 54–55, 111
carbon 16
carbon cycle 29
carbon dioxide 10, 15, 16, 18, 19,
	20, 22, 28, 29, 31, 58, 83, 93,
	100, 103
carbon emissions 19, 20, 31, 100,
	102, 103, 105
carbon footprint 31, 93, 101, 103,
	104
central heating 19
chemicals 21, 44, 45, 47, 76
child labour 112
cities 90, 94, 95, 109
climate 7
climate change 7, 15, 87, 100,
	110, 114
	effects of 22–25, 87
	slowing down 28, 30
climate zones 8–9, 23
clothes 106, 112
coal 15, 16, 17, 41, 93, 98, 99
combine harvesters 63, 76
conservation 42, 57, 58, 111
coral reefs 34, 47, 56, 58
corn 66, 82
cows 20, 49, 63, 78, 79
crabeater seals 37
crops 31, 44, 45, 49, 62, 64, 66, 69
	crop rotation 77
cycling 103

deserts 8, 9, 23, 34, 38, 95
diesel 16, 98
diseases 13, 86, 109
domesticated animals 63
	see also livestock
droughts 6, 24, 25, 87

Earth Hour (2009) 115
ecological footprint 92
ecotourism 52
electricity 14, 19, 30, 36, 93, 98,
	101, 105
electric vehicles 103
elephants 34, 44
El Niño 23
endangered species 35, 51, 54, 81,
	110, 111
energy 19, 28, 91, 92, 97, 98, 102,
	104, 105, 107
	alternative energy sources
	30, 101
	energy efficiency 14, 19, 21,
	29, 93, 104, 105
Equator 8, 9
ethanol 82
extinction 35, 59, 71

factories 19, 91, 92, 96, 97, 108
fairtrade 112–113
farmers' markets 31, 85
farming 22, 23, 36, 44–45, 59,
	60–87, 95, 113
	biofuel production 31
	factory farming 64
	farm animals 22, 37, 44, 49,
	63, 64, 65, 66, 78–79
	organic 77
	see also crops
fish farming 81
fishing 22, 23, 36, 44, 45, 59,
	80–81, 110
floods 6, 13, 23, 24, 25, 26, 73,
	87, 100
flowering plants 13
food 90, 92, 94, 108–109
	fairtrade 112
	fast food 109
	food aid 86, 87
	food miles 85
	food mountains 84
	food waste 109
	and health problems 109
	production 108
	see also farming
footprints 92–93, 105
forests 69, 70, 74
	see also trees; tropical forests
fossil fuels 15, 16–17, 18, 19, 30,
	83, 87, 98, 99, 102, 114
fossils 16–17, 35

free-range animals 79
fruit orchards 66
fuels 16, 18–19, 58, 82, 85, 92, 93,
	98–99, 102
	burning 15, 18, 19, 30, 31, 58,
	87, 93, 98, 100, 102
	fossil 15, 16–17, 18, 19, 30,
	83, 87, 98, 99, 102, 114
	non-fossil 99

gadgets 93, 105
genetically modified (GM) crops 79
geothermal energy 101
giant pandas 35, 50, 54
glaciers 13, 27
global footprint 93, 101, 102, 108,
	111, 114, 115
global warming 12–13, 85, 110
	causes 20, 58, 87, 93, 100
	effects 13, 15, 26–27, 87, 100
	reducing 28–29, 30, 31, 83
grasslands 34, 44, 66
Great Barrier Reef 56
great white sharks 34
greenhouse effect 10–11, 14
greenhouse gases 10, 14, 15, 16,
	19, 20–21, 58, 83, 100
'green' product labels 97
'green' transport 103
guinea pigs 65

habitats 38–39, 50, 95
	habitat loss 22, 37, 40–41, 49,
	70, 72, 75, 76, 83, 110
headline species 50–51
heatwaves 24, 25
homes 90, 98, 104–105
hunter-gatherers 62
hurricanes 6, 24, 25, 100
hybrid cars 103
hydroelectricity 30, 101

Ice Ages 7
icebergs 13, 27, 34, 58
industries 96, 97, 115
insects 13
introduced species 48–49

Komodo dragons 50

landfills 20, 21
livestock 63, 64, 65, 66, 78–79
low-energy light bulbs 93

Index

metals 97
methane 20, 82
migration 75
mining 41, 97, 98
mobile phones 92
monkeys 45, 53, 55, 71
moose (elk) 43
mountain gorillas 50, 51, 58

natural gas 15, 16, 17, 20, 93, 98, 99
nature reserves and wildlife parks 42–43, 54, 55, 111
nuclear energy 30

oceans and seas 22, 26, 34, 38, 43, 47, 80–81
oil 16, 17, 19, 92, 93, 96, 98, 99
oil rigs 17, 96
oil spills 47
orang-utans 34, 50, 59
ores 97
organic farming 77
overfishing 80
oxygen 14, 21, 28, 29
ozone 20, 21

paper 19, 68, 107
parrots 53
pelicans 75
penguins 39
pests 48, 49, 76, 77, 79, 84
pet animals 52, 53
petrol 15, 16, 98, 101
photosynthesis 28
planes 19, 90, 99, 103, 108
plastics 19, 92, 96, 106, 107
poachers 59
polar bears 34, 54, 58
polar climate 7, 9
pollution 46–47, 58, 85, 97, 107, 110
    air 19, 21, 36, 91, 102, 103
    soil 76
    water 42, 46–47, 76, 111
population growth 36, 63, 64, 89, 94–95
power stations 14, 19, 30, 36, 91, 93, 98

radioactive waste 30
rainforests 8, 38, 70
    see also tropical forests
raw materials 21, 90, 91, 96–97, 102, 105, 106
recycling 21, 41, 107, 114
Red List 51
red spotted newts 111
repairing and re-using items 106, 107
rhinos 7, 51, 54, 55
rice 45, 62, 65, 74

sea levels, rising 13, 26–27
smog 21
snow and ice 6, 7, 13, 27
soil 66, 67, 77
    erosion 72, 73, 74
solar panels 101
soya crops 73, 82, 83
standby mode 93
starvation 86, 109
storms 6, 23, 24, 87
sustainable resources 69, 71, 83, 99, 101

temperate climate 8
temperatures 9, 11, 12, 15, 22, 58
tigers 35, 50, 55
timber/wood 15, 41, 59, 68, 69, 70, 71, 72, 93, 99
tourism 52–53, 56, 57
transport 84, 85, 101, 102–103, 108
    'green' transport 103
    public transport 103
travel miles 31
trees 29, 31, 41, 58, 68–71, 72, 76
tropical climate 7, 8, 9
tropical forests 8, 34, 38, 41, 52, 56, 58, 70, 71, 72, 73, 83
tropical hardwoods 70
turtles 47, 52, 53, 81

vehicles 90, 97, 98, 99, 102, 103
Venus 11

waste 20, 21, 46, 90, 109
    reducing 106–107
water
    saving 104, 107
    shortages 22, 23, 44
water hyacinth 48
water vapour 14, 15
weather 6, 7
weather balloons 15
weather stations 12
wells 22
wetlands 75
whales 50, 52
wind energy 30, 101
winds 6, 9, 24, 25
woolly mammoths 7
workers 112, 113

Yangtze river dolphins 59